COLLABORATING FOR SUCCESS:
THE FUTURE OF IT SERVICE
AND SUPPORT CULTURE

Collaborating for Success: The Future of IT Service and Support Culture

©2019 By Bob Roark

ISBN Paperback: 9781912651566
ISBN eBook: 9781912651573

First Published in Great Britain by ITSM Shop Ltd

Other Best Practice Press Publications:

A Guide to Lean
A Concise Introduction to DevOps
A Concise Introduction to Project Management

Best Practice Press
95 Duxford Road,
Whittlesford, Cambs,
CB22 4NJ,
UK
+44 (0) 3333 445 286
customerservices@bestpracticepress.com
www.bestpracticepress.com

CONTENTS

INTRODUCTION

Over the last twenty years of working within IT Service and Support, I have noticed a disconnect between different IT departments and end users, so have attempted solutions to break down the walls between these groups in order to provide a more valuable experience for customers. While individual efforts in addressing these disconnects have bridged the gap to a significant degree, they are even more noticeable today than they were back then.

The challenge facing IT

The challenges of providing excellent customer value in relation to IT are still as prevalent today as they have been for the last 20 years. IT groups are operating in their own worlds, working hard to provide value, but not looking at IT Service Management (ITSM) as an end-to-end solution for their users. This means they accomplish their own tasks at the cost of conflicting with customer interests or organization of the company.

Additionally, there appeared to be a discord between the IT department and the Operations team. This is further heightened within Operations themselves, Tier 3 (e.g. System Administration), felt more superior than Tier 2 (e.g. Desktop Support) and Tier 1 (e.g. Help Desk), believing them to be less competent and professional. Tier 2 did the same to Tier 1 for the same reasons, while Tier 1 just wanted to provide customer service and collaborate with the other teams to achieve the end goal.

In the early 2000s, I was introduced to ITIL®, originally known then as the Information Technology Infrastructure Library, rebranded today as simply ITIL. ITIL provided a common language for everyone and showed a methodical way to provide IT services to customers. I felt it was the answer to address the disconnects we were experiencing between the different IT groups (e.g. Development, Help Desk, Desktop Support, System Administration, etc.). I jumped on board with ITIL, trained my staff and began adopting and adapting different processes in order to be consistent and provide a stable and more effective work environment. ITIL was successful for the Help Desk and eventually Desktop Support, but, didn't seem to take hold with the other groups in IT, especially on the development side of the house.

As time went by, different methodologies, business models and practices that met the needs of specific groups became the norm. Development teams adopted the Capability Maturity Model Integration (CMMI®), a process level training improvement and appraisal program developed at Carnegie Mellon University (CMU), Agile software development, and LeanIT process improvement. Project Managers took on the Project Management Institute® (PMI®) Body of Knowledge (PMBOK®) framework and Agile project management methods, while Operations embraced the ITIL and LeanIT.

Disputes between the groups continued: Tier 1 became the voice of the customer to other IT groups, but was still only viewed as entry level. Development felt that Operations were making the process too stringent and slow, while Operations felt that Development were too fast and lacked control, creating a system impossible to support. Then a few years ago, a change began to emerge: Finances were reformed, and organizations started pushing IT to provide services at a cheaper rate. This opened the door to revamping by moving services and support to the cloud. In short, the cloud would allow companies to reduce their overhead of both capital and staffing costs by providing a standard set of infrastructure, platform, and software as service (SaaS) options. It took some time for cloud services to work out the bugs and gain buy-in from organizations, but since then it has grown extremely fast. This also encouraged the need for DevOps, a methodology that combines Development and Operations by breaking down silos using an automating software, which in turn provides value to customers in a swift and economical fashion.

Even with all of the frameworks, methodologies, and models in place, organizations are still struggling with the same group dynamic issues that I observed back in the early 2000s. In fact, they are worse today because of the fear of new methods erasing jobs, however, this can't be further from the truth. The problem is that IT are not really looking at their products and services from an end-to-end perspective driven by a customer-centric culture, or ensuring that their teams and organizations are able to adapt to change. Instead of trying to implement a monolithic single system, teams are not communicating with each other in order to utilize their individual strengths to deliver optimal results. The truth is, there is no singular framework that can do it all.

The Solution

The good news is, everything we need to succeed is already in place. With ITIL at its core, Integrated Service Management™ (ISM™) frameworks, practices, and models (ITIL, LeanIT, Agile, DevOps, and Organizational Change Management) are complementary to each other, providing a collaborative approach to technical service and support for both now and the future.

Simply put, ISM is using current IT business models in a way that plays on each strength to ensure value to the customer, while meeting current and future challenges.

ISM is an IT service management methodology that brings together different aspects of existing management practices to achieve more accurate results, faster delivery, and reduced costs of services, ultimately creating user satisfaction at a greater value. These build on and are complementary to each other, providing a collaborative approach to technical service and support, for both now and the future. Benefits of ISM include:

- Improved requirements generation
- Improved business value
- Improved delivery speed
- Reduced costs and complexity
- Improved collaboration
- Flattening the organization
- Achieving a culture without (or reduced) silos

There are six main components to ISM - ITIL, LeanIT, Agile, DevOps, Organizational Change Management, and Customer Experience (CX). ITIL provides a common language and central structure for the success of the integration of all other technology frameworks and business models. LeanIT encourages a continual service improvement function and Agile provides project management. DevOps, at the writing of this book, is the new kid on the block (probably the most misunderstood), and provides two things. First, it breaks down the communication barriers between all the groups inside of IT, and second, it provides automation for application development as technology progresses to the cloud. Organizational Change Management focuses on change from a people perspective rather than a technological one. And finally, CX encourages IT organizations to focus on a customer-centric culture to truly understand their needs. All of these frameworks, business models, processes and standards work together to provide value to the customer.

Who is this book for?

While this book has a lot of useful information that may appeal to a range of audiences, my primary goal was to concentrate on IT Executives, Directors, Managers, and staff in both the operations and development sides of IT.

What you will get out of this book

This book will give you a general understanding of Service Management, IT Service Management, IT Service Delivery and ISM as a model, while providing tactical advice on how to begin as well as mature your ITSM integration journey. In this context, Service Management is an organizational level approach looking at the end-to-end view rather than focusing on a single department (such as IT, HR, Finance, etc.), that helps organizations to respond to their consumers and deliver value with integrated service management practices. IT Service Management (IT only) is, therefore, a subset of Service Management and is a framework that provides best practices for aligning IT and business needs to provide value to IT's customer. Service Delivery then, is the tactical application and implementation of Service Management and/or IT Service Management frameworks, functions, best practices and related activities that produce specific outcomes resulting in value to customers from their perspective.

While I will cover some of today's popular methods, the goal of this book is not to train the reader to be an expert in any one specific framework, methodology or business model used in IT, ITSM or ISM. There are many fine organizations and specific publications that can help the reader achieve a deeper understanding of these techniques. Additionally, if you are so inclined, there is a certification for ISM that can be obtained from Professional Designations and Pink Elephant. Therefore, the intent of this book is to give the reader an overview of what these frameworks are, what they do best, and how they can (and must) work together to achieve the greatest success in responding to the current challenges of providing IT services, better *AND* faster *AND* cheaper.

Chapter 1 – How Did We Get Here?

This chapter discusses the problems facing the state of IT, a brief history of the iterations and structures that led to the current state, why we need ISM, and the benefits.

Chapter 2 – Meeting Customer's Expectations

This chapter discusses customer expectations (what they really are, eliciting them, etc.) and introduces the Customer Experience (CX), Voice of the Customer (VOC), Customer Journey Mapping and Value Stream Mapping.

Chapter 3 – Frameworks, Models and processes

This chapter discusses the main IT Service Management frameworks, practices and models involved with ISM, with a brief synopsis for each. The goal is to give the reader a basic understanding, not a detailed knowledge transfer. We will also discuss why knowing each in greater detail is needed.

Chapter 4 – Standards, Models and Best Practices

This chapter discusses a few other standards and the best practices involved with a brief synopsis for each. This includes the likes of HDI®, ISO, ISACA®

COBIT®, NIST®, etc. The goal is to give the reader a basic understanding, not a detailed knowledge transfer. We will also discuss why knowing each in greater detail is needed.

Chapter 5 – Future of ITSM

This chapter discusses why IT needs to change, what the drives is and what the structure of IT will look like in the future. The goal is to understand the urgency and excitement of moving to a mature ISM environment.

Chapter 6 – Communication for Everyone

This chapter discusses why communication early and often is so important. We will discuss Customer, Team, Management, Peer, and change communication. The goal is to understand the multiple levels of communication and perceptions to assist in asking the right thing, to the right people, at the right time.

Chapter 7 – A Winning Strategy for Integrating ITSM

This chapter discusses how to gain upper management buy-in to successfully mature the organizational culture, discuss specific How To's (e.g. Process, Meetings, and Assessments, etc.), and provide Continual Service Improvement (CSI).

CHAPTER 1:

HOW DID WE GET HERE?

A Brief History of IT Support

Information Technology (IT) has been around for as long as humans themselves have, driven by the desire to communicate. From cave drawings to our current digital age, the one constant with IT is that it has never stopped evolving. The focus of this book is the most recent iteration in the digital age of computing from a business perspective rather than a technological one. The digital age of IT is still comparatively young, and encompasses a wide range of products and services developed over time to help process calculations and data, replacing manual systems for a better, faster and cheaper business mode.

Prior to the inception of the digital age of IT, the evolution of a market could have taken decades or longer to develop to full maturity. For example, grocery stores today did not start out as mega-stores. They started small, individual proprietor owned operations providing only necessary items to consumers who were just around the corner. This model was in place for over one hundred years, and while effective for their current customers, these stores lacked a variety of goods to widen their consumer audience. Growth was also imperative for other industries as they intertwined, and a demand for easy products and services emerged. In the grocery store example, as the automotive industry grew, so did the ability for these local customers to travel to other areas to get different products. Consumers could now easily travel further from their homes to procure goods and services. This new- found availability reduced the revenue of the small stores, and in response to the new demand, many combined their efforts and consolidated their offerings into a larger, more cost-effective model. This eventually evolved into the super mega supermarkets of today. At the writing of this book, even these mega-stores are experiencing the beginnings of the next change in demand and availability with the advent of online shopping for grocery delivery.

As with other industries, IT has grown and developed, but at a comparatively accelerated pace. The major influence in the rapid growth is down to technology assisting in the development and advancement of other industries. These other industries either wanted or needed technology to further their own progress, increase profits and maintain their competitiveness. The rapid pace of IT evolution has facilitated many underlying weaknesses for both IT Operations and IT Development business units.

At the start, other industries did not care about many standard IT business practices because they wanted the competitive edge that IT products and rapid pace for delivery provided. This practice made IT an 800lb Gorilla, and we have been in a very reactive mode ever since. Back then, money was almost thrown at IT without regard, the maxim at the time was "pay more, get it faster, and damn the consequences". This lack of regard and rapid growth gave a false sense of confidence to those in IT.

As the pendulum swung back from the fast-paced and weak business custom of IT to that of standard practice, areas such as cost and governance, where once ignored to one degree or another, rapidly became of greater concern. One of the first areas that were significantly affected was the "bottom falling out" of the internet, known as the Dot-com bust, which occurred between 1995 and 2000. In this event, many internet-only based companies were overvalued merely because they were interesting. Investors were overly excited to jump on board with promises of making easy money. During the internet boom, many companies made decisions to invest in and build their organizations in ways that disregarded standard business practices in order to deliver products and services. These companies quickly found out (and too late in many cases) that they could not simply ignore these standard business practices. As many businesses didn't see their revenues grow as expected, investors backed out and the businesses began to fail en masse resulting in a slump of revenue of internet-only businesses.

Today, IT is still trying hard to align itself with standard business practices, just like other segments (e.g. accounting, legal, purchasing, facilities, etc.) have been doing for decades.

The Problem with IT Support Models

The beginning models of IT service and support started with programmers creating an application to perform specific functions with a very technical manual to match. When users of the application would have technical issues, they would call the programmers directly to get assistance. These programmers were more concerned with managing existing applications and creating new ones, rather than providing customer service to end-users. Their responses were often laced with annoyance and consisted of the question "have you read the manual?" Additionally, these developers were considered a very expensive resource, so having them answer basic customer inquiries instead of focusing on creating new or maintaining existing applications was not benefiting either the companies or the users.

Once businesses figured out that they were spending unnecessary time answering phone calls rather than creating new programs, management decided to move the "support call" function from programmer to a secretary. Companies soon found that customers were not being responded to at all because the secretaries (having limited technical knowledge) would simply take a message and pass it on to the programmers. Customers inquiries went unanswered because programmers were both too busy working on applications, and also did not want to talk interact with them. They were under pressure to write new programs, and besides, all of the customer questions could easily be answered in the wonderful manual (and programmers knew it was wonderful because after all, they wrote it) that was distributed with the product anyway.

During this time, and with the lack of response from programmers, some secretaries began to read the manuals and became significantly more proficient with the application than others. They became the "go to" in their office for questions on the program as users did not want to read the book or were intimidated by the technology.

Eventually, companies gathered up these "advanced users" and created an internal IT department, because there was no budget or office space for this type of endeavor, most of these departments began in closets, basements or boiler rooms. As time progressed these individuals became more knowledgeable across all lines of IT, they focused their attention on what they were most adept at (e.g. application development, database administration, system administration, desktop support, etc.), each spending their time on their specific modality. The time and focus problem described earlier that occurred with the application developers also extended to this group of specialists as well. The more compartmentalized a person became, the further away from the consumer they were, thus perpetuating more groups and increasingly frustrated customers. Users of the technology were wanting better IT support, but as the technology was new and somewhat intimidating, the norm became accepting whatever IT would give them. Due to the limited time to help with issues and inquiries, companies developed a help desk to assist customers.

The first help desks were viewed as a stepping stone for individuals with limited knowledge in IT, who wanted to get their foot in the door and eventually progress to a more specialized arena (e.g. system administration, programming, database administration, etc.).

One of the first issues that occurred was the specialized IT staff withholding activities, rights, and capabilities from the newly formed help desk, both to avoid disruptive actions by staff who were not seen as capable, and to also protect their own jobs. The problem that arose from this model was that companies could not keep knowledgeable individuals who had the ability to solve technological issues in direct contact with the customers. While this model facilitated technology growth and stability, the model diminished customer interactions, resulting in user dissatisfaction with IT in general. At this point, they started to hear terms like "helpless desk", etc.

Over the past several years, a progression has been made to move away from help desks to a more technically savvy and highly professional single point of contact, focused solely on customer service. This focus has changed from one in which technology was implemented merely for the sake of it regardless of whether it was helpful to the user, to a customer-centric model where their needs are the driving force for the development of products and services. This has been a challenge because of the substantial changes all those involved, including customers, IT management and every level in between. Furthermore, studies have shown that CX will be the number one drive for customers doing business with a company in the near future.

Although businesses and IT departments are slowly making a move toward a customer-centric IT support model, implementing it does come with challenges. One of the more important being the uncertainty of what practices work best. Another is educating current (IT as well as organizational) management and staff on how teams should work to facilitate customer value and experience. Suffice to say, there are some major challenges ahead with regard to CX and its role in the future of IT.

Team structure

Organizational structure is the system used to define the hierarchy of a business and its job roles, functions and reporting. There are four main organizational structures used today: Functional, Divisional, Matrix, and Flatarchy, each with a specific purpose used for many years.

Functional organization structures are designed as a top-down hierarchical structure in which everyone eventually reports to the CEO (see Figure 1). Jobs and functions are broken into departments and groups, which are banded together in a logical order. For example, a Finance Department may contain Sales, Marketing, and Accounting groups. This is the most typical and basic structure used today.

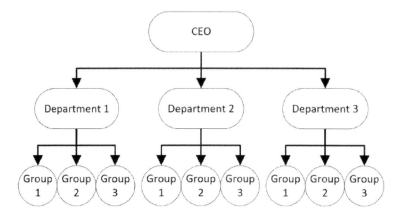

Figure 1: Functional Organizational Structure

Divisional organizational structures (see Figure 2) are similar to Functional groups generally used by larger businesses. They have similar reporting structures, however the divisional structure allows each group to operate as its own company. For example, an organization with an Eastern and Western region may decide to break its business into separate divisions. Each of these Divisions then runs its business separately from the other.

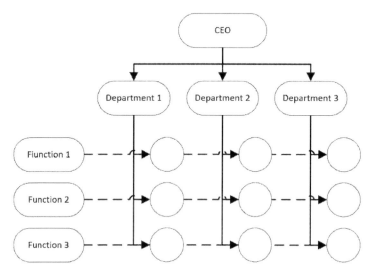

Figure 2: Divisional Organizational Structure

Matrix organizational structures are a hybrid, combining jobs and groups of the Functional organizational structure with specific project-based activities (see Figure 3). For example, an IT organization's Operations, Development and Governance Departments may combine their staff members delivery and support efforts to utilize resources across all teams regardless of the specific reporting structure.

There are challenges with Matrix organization structures, specifically staff members having multiple managers, who conflict with each other on things like time allocation, delivery, etc. I remember a time during one of my first IT support jobs, I was part of Operations, and because of my personal expertise and experience, was also asked to work in the Development department for an enterprise website. My direct manager's boss oversaw the website development effort and asked to have me assigned to the project, and I excitedly agreed. After a few months of working on both the IT Operations support team and the IT Developments website project, I received my annual performance appraisal from my direct supervisor. In the review, my supervisor expressed his concerns with my availability to the IT Operations team and graded me as below the standard required by my primary job. I was surprised by the grade as I had been working many hours of (required) overtime, had not missed any scheduled shifts for either group and received many kudos from both the IT Operations team and the IT Development project team, managers and customers. When I asked about the score, the supervisor explained that what caused the low grades was that my work on the IT Development teams project was not his primary concern and that he had to work around my required project schedule. I learned two lessons from that experience. First, whichever manager the employee is closet to in the daily work activities, wins. Second, managers may resent sharing their team members in a matrix managed environment. The Matrix model sounds good on paper, but as long as there are conflicting managerial demands, staff members will have difficulty pleasing all managers involved.

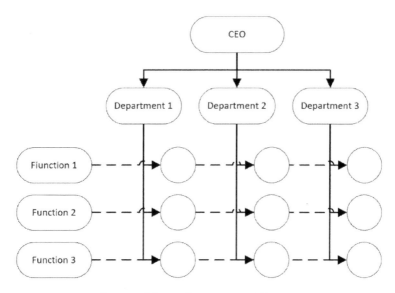

Figure 3: Matrix Organizational Structure

Flatarchy organizational models, as you might have guessed by the name, is a hybrid (see Figure 4) combining the hierarchical and functional models. These organizations strive to flatten the levels of authority in an organization to allow a more agile managerial structure by removing roadblocks that slow the decision-making process. One of the major advantages of the Flatarchy model is that it works to limit silo-based knowledge and increase speed in completing activities (e.g. projects and services). A challenge with this model however, is gaining buying from existing organizational structures who feel loss or encroachment upon their fiefdoms.

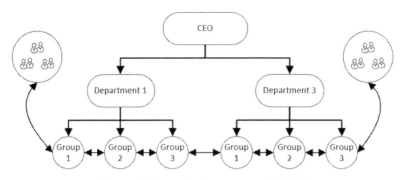

Figure 4: Flatarchy Organizational Model

Since the business is designed using these organizational structures, it only makes sense that IT followed these modes. While this standard business model does make sense reporting from the top down, it divides the groups into silos of information, resource, and ability (see Figure 5). These silos then separate group directions and drive a wedge between the groups and their teams. DevOps further defines this as the Wall of Confusion, where at a fundamental level, neither the Operations or the Development teams understands why, what or how the other is doing business, resulting in a lack of cohesion between teams in providing value to the business.

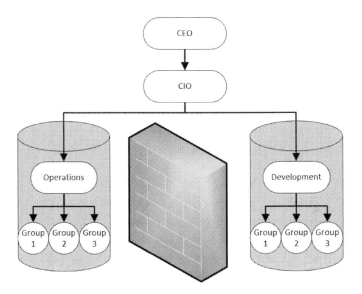

Figure 5: IT Silos and Wall of Confusion

The issue with breaking teams into structures of a standard business model is that they don't work together or no what each group is trying to accomplish. This makes them all work toward completing their own goals in their own ways, thus duplicating efforts in some areas.

Better, Faster, Cheaper

You have no doubt heard the old adage, "better, faster, or cheaper, you can pick any two, but not all three." IT is fantastic at the better and faster pieces, we have these down to a science. But it's the cheaper aspect that has become the biggest concern as of late. IT often echoes "do more with less. This is not an exact or entirely accurate description of what is needed. It would be better to rephrase it as "do more *by* doing less".

Doing less. What does that really mean? It is not suggesting to provide less quality, especially as the workload is ever-increasing in volume and complexity. Doing more by doing less encourages organizations to look at the duplication of effort and reduce that. Silos are not conducive to doing less, the duplication in many areas still exist. If we integrate the teams in a way that allows each group to do what they are best at, activities can be delegated across the teams. For example, every group does some form of change management, but each in their own way and within their own timeframes. What if we could shift the structure of these activities to the teams that do the job best.

ITIL also describes three types of changes (Normal, Standard, and Emergency), each of which have their own process. Since ITIL is non-prescriptive, any of its defined processes can be adopted or adapted to suit the needs of the specific organization. Historically, many practitioners have misinterpreted ITIL's non-prescriptive direction as "all or nothing" and when adopting a specific process for their organization, followed the ITIL guidelines to the letter without regard for their organization's rules, regulations and culture.

For change management, ITIL describes starting with a change request that is passed on to change management for approval, which could include engagement with a change advisory board (CAB). According to ITIL, the CAB is "a group of people that support the assessment, prioritization, authorization, and scheduling of changes" (AXELOS, ITIL Service Design), who by the way, may only meet occasionally. Furthermore, the CAB acts as definitive change authority in some organizations, or an advisory body in others. In either case, any requests, escalations or interactions with the CAB can elongate the process cycle.

Where change management comes into play, these "all or nothing" misinterpretations have resulted in a very formal change approval process, whether they are necessary or not. This has resulted in the need for almost everything to go through a long and arduous formal procedure, making the entire affair very slow and cumbersome.

Complicating things further, even where a change management process was adopted, not every group has followed their company's definitive change practice. Instead, they utilized a separate process which worked for their specific group regardless of the impact or engagement with others. For example, Agile teams have a compressed version of the ITIL change management process, combining and pre-approve a lot of the activities to ensure that changes can be made quickly. While every group builds off of the ITIL management process, the way they actually make a change may not be the same. Issues therefore arise when one group's criteria for change does not match another's criteria or requirements, leading to ineffective functioning and a lack of cohesion.

If we can take the best of the change management process from the group that is doing it in the fastest, cheapest and most effective way, and adopt that across all teams, we can accomplish the desire for a "cheaper service". This scales across all areas of IT as well. If we adopt and adapt ITIL as the standard language, LeanIT as the process improvement, Agile as the project management, DevOps as the development automation guided by organizational change management and CX management, we can reduce the duplication of effort and thus the associated cost.

It is all about having the right people, doing the right things at the right time in a standard way across and in conjunction with *all* IT teams. This is the high level of sophistication ISM brings and why it is the future of how we provide value through IT services and products.

In the beginning, siloed based teams were naturally formed to perform specific functions. The attempt to help customers quickly and efficiently, and not bombarding technicians and programmers with customer queries made sense. Over time however, this goal had unintentionally become an extensive problem for both IT and their customers. By separating the groups, IT has built teams that don't talk to each other and worse yet, don't always have the end user's best interests at heart. Sure, if you talk to any IT individual, regardless of their team or function, they will say "I am doing all that I can to meet customer demands. In fact, if we could just get (INSERT WHICHEVER IT GROUP NAME YOU DESIRE HERE) to understand what we are doing and why, everything would work better for everyone."

If all the groups have these same thoughts, why is that we are still faced with these ongoing issues? In the end, everyone wants to get to the same place, just using different directions, thoughts and pressures to get there. As I described earlier, DevOps appropriately defines this problem as The Wall of Confusion. Groups know what their job is and assume that everyone else knows too, but the more siloed a group is, the larger the misunderstandings their group has of others and vice versa. That is not to say that each group is not doing what they should, just that when working in a vacuum, groups cannot see the bigger picture of how and why everything needs to work together to achieve the end goal.

Another effect of siloed teams is that they adopt practices designed as end-to-end solutions for themselves, without taking other teams into account, resulting in duplicating efforts. For example, every group in IT has a specific process for improvement or change management. Unfortunately, many of the processes are not aligned with each other, even though in the end they all want the same things. This duplication works inside their silo, but when products or services are eventually transferred to other groups, who by the way are operating in the same manner, doesn't match their requirements in accordance with their own group. This chain of duplication goes on and on throughout the lifecycle of all products and services, resulting in frustration from teams and eventually the customers. Remember that in the end, the customer only knows IT as a single entity and does not care about the innerworkings of the groups, as long as they receive the support they need. When they call the service desk or a programmer/system administrator, they see them as IT, not a separate silo and expect that the person knows and represents every aspect. As you can well imagine, not knowing what other groups do or how can result in any person that is engaging with customers giving incorrect, inaccurate or non-attainable advice.

What is your job anyway?

Some years ago, I attended a meeting with staff from the IT support groups including Tier 1 (service desk), Tier 2 (desktop support) and Tier 3 (system administration) IT Operations groups. We were all there to talk about how to better meet customer needs. As the meeting began, I heard complaints from the different groups. Tier 1 would complain that Tier 2 and Tier 3 didn't trust them with the correct information or didn't give them the rights for access to accomplish what the customers asked them to do. Tier 3 would in turn say "when something's escalated from Tier 1 or Tier 2 to Tier 3, they don't provide the correct information in the ticket". Tier 1 or 2 would then turn to Tier 3 and say "what do you want to know? Help us understand what it is you're asking for so that we can give it to you", Tier 3 would be standoffish and not provide the information. After a few minutes of watching these teams go back and forth complaining about the lack of communication with each other, I stopped the meeting and asked them what they thought their jobs were. The responses that I received were very interesting. I heard a lot of "I'm a Service Desk agent" or "I'm a Desktop Support Technician" or "I'm a SharePoint® Administrator a Network Administrator". I said, "that's what you do, but what's your job?" They looked at me a bit puzzled and I replied, "our job is to facilitate an outcome for the customer. How we provide that is through all of these technologies that you're talking about. If you don't believe me, then tell me, what is the network operating system that you're currently working on right now? Is it the same one that you started out with in your career 10 or 15 years ago? My guess is that the answer is no. There's probably 2, 3, or even more different network operating system iterations that you've worked with during that period time. So, it's not so much the networking technology itself, your job is facilitating and outcome by utilizing network administration." To the desktop support agents I said, "look at how many different types of desktops you need to work on. What kind of formats are you dealing with? Are they still the same things that you worked with at the beginning of your career?" Then I asked the group, "for those of you that been around for a while, has that technology changed? We have seen technology change from green screen AS/400's, XT, 386, 486, Pentium®, Pentium II, Pentium III, Pentium 4, etc., desktops, laptops, tablets, smartphones, etc. These are the technologies that we use to facilitate an outcome for the customer, not the job itself." The content of this meeting has been an ongoing conversation for all of my staff over the years. In summary, our job in IT then becomes something in which we really need to look at from a customer's perspective in getting them back to work and keeping them as productive as possible, as fast as possible.

At all levels, teams and groups, we really work hard to provide IT services and support, but unfortunately, because the work is ever evolving and teams are broken into silos, customers are often forgotten. We forget that we are providing something to the customer to allow them to accomplish something for their business needs. From a customer's perspective, the value is entirely what they think it is. So, if they think it's good, it's good. If they think it's bad, it's bad. What are our jobs and what are we here for? The short answer is that we are here to provide value for our customers by doing whatever it takes, IT is a facilitator of that activity, not the activity in and of itself.

Next Steps

The world is changing. Today's IT organizations know they must transform to not only thrive but survive. With services moving to the cloud, consolidation efforts and organizations pushing to make the already better and faster products and services cheaper as well, IT organizations must find ways to do more, by doing less. This is where Service Management comes into play.

Service Management is a term to encompass all the groups throughout an organization, including Human Resources, Financial Management, Facilities

Management and IT (see Figure 7) to support the best practices, processes and regulations specific to each.

Enterprise Service Management (ESM) is an approach used to look at the end-to-end view rather than focusing on a single department (such as IT, HR, Finance, Facilities, etc.), that helps organizations respond to their consumers and deliver value with ESM practices across all lines of business.

In the past, those of us in IT had an understanding that Service Management was delivery, but as organizations have matured, it has become clear that IT is only part of Service Management. Today's world is beginning to evolve from these separate groups being directly under the specific business area, they are supporting (see Figure 6) to an ESM model (Figure 7). At the writing of this book, ESM is at the beginning stages of being adopted by organizations, however, it is unclear how or when exactly this will take place.

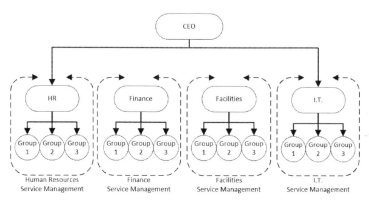

Figure 6: Current Service Management Organization Structure Example

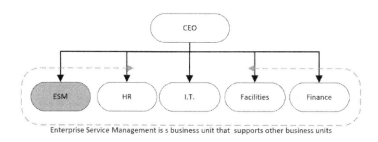

Figure 7: Enterprise Service Management Example

27

For the context of this book, I will be discussing IT Service Management as a model that will continue to work both under the current IT and future ESM management structures. Let's define the components of Service Management as it relates to IT.

IT Service Management: A subset of Service Management. This is a framework that provides the best practices for aligning IT with business needs in order to provide value to the customer. It consists of Strategy, Design, Transition, Operations, and Continual Service Improvement. Value is whatever a customer perceives it to be.

IT Service Delivery: The tactical application and implementation of Service Management and IT Service Management frameworks, functions, best practices and related activities that produce specific outcomes resulting in value to customers from their perspective.

IT Service Delivery is therefore the tactical action of delivering and continuously increasing value to customers in a mutually beneficial and profitable way. In order to achieve this, we need to understand the customer and their desires in much greater detail than ever before. The next chapter describes the customer's expectations (what they really are, eliciting them, etc.) and introduces the Customer Experience (CX), Voice of the Customer (VOC), Customer Journey Mapping and Value Stream Mapping.

Key Takeaways

- IT has evolved beyond normal business structure and silos. To ensure success, they must break these silos down and ensure everyone is working towards the same goal.
- Eliminating the Wall of Confusion between teams is necessary to provide better *AND* faster *AND* cheaper IT products and services to customers,
- Service Management is larger than just IT.

CHAPTER 2:

MEETING CUSTOMER'S EXPECTATIONS

Customers

Depending on who you talk to or what framework you are adhering to, there are a lot of different definitions for who a customer actually is. Additionally, depending on the specific framework or business model you are working in, the terms may be different, the same or have an entirely different definition altogether. For the purposes of this book, I define a customer as the requester, decision maker, purchaser, business itself and/or the consumer of a product or service.

Value

Value is whatever the customer perceives it to be. Whatever the customer believes, in their minds, is the only thing that matters. There are a lot of frameworks, policies, procedures, and group functions that exist in today's IT world. We have worked very hard over time in making our specific groups and processes function well, regardless of what the customer actually wanted or needed.

Imagine, if you will, you wanted to order a pizza. You, as the customer, know you want a pizza and that's it. Why is it important for the pizzeria to understand what you really want? I mean after all its just a pizza, right? Maybe, but most likely you do have certain expectations and probably some that you are not even aware of. What if you have dietary constraints and you want a gluten-free pizza, but the pizzeria owner didn't know and never offered that choice. You would not get your pizza at their establishment. What if the pizzeria knew, because they asked you, why you never bought pizza from them, and you explained you needed a gluten-free option? They could then decide to add that to their menu, and you might become a customer. You are looking at the value of that pizza too, you may think $20 for a pizza is good value for money, but what if the pizzeria was charging $30, $40 or $50 for a pizza. Would that change your mind?

The customer's perception of value changes over time as well. Professor Noriaki Kano describes this drift in detail in his Kano Theory Model (see Figure 8: Kano Model).

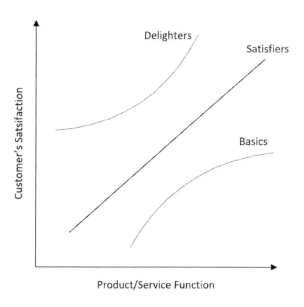

Figure 8: Kano Model

The Kano model classifies customer preference attributes into Basic (must haves), Satisfiers (want to have) and Delighters (nice to have). Over time the Delighters become Satisfiers and the Satisfiers become the Basics. This can be exemplified if you look back on cellular telecommunications. In the beginning, a dial tone was the Basic attribute. The ability to travel between cities in a car or train and maintain the call was a Satisfier and the ability to integrate email and calendar appointments was a Delighter. As you can imagine, in today's world this is a much different picture. The integration of all mobile device computing, once a delighter, is now a Satisfier or a Basic on the Kano model chart. This drift of satisfaction is important to remember because it never stops, and we need to remember to continually check in with customers to make sure we are meeting their expectations on all levels.

Every single person has their own definition of what value is to them. Because organizations are made of different individuals, it stands to reason that every organization's specific statement for requirements will have many nuances about what actual success looks like.

Expectations

Not focusing on what the customers actually wanted may have worked for us in the past, but as we move forward customers are demanding more than just reactionarily providing products and services without thinking about functionality. I am not suggesting that the past is wasted or has not provided any value to users whatsoever, but as times change, so do the customers' expectations. Not only do they expect us to deliver what we always have, but they also want us to bring new solutions for things they do not even know yet, all in a better *AND* faster *AND* cheaper way. I was working with a CIO recently, who when asked what he wanted, replied: "I don't really know, but I will know it when I see it." This kind of response makes our position in IT very difficult. How do we provide something that we can't even define? The direction from the customer, while not always clear in its details, is very adamant, however, "give me what I want even before I know what I need."

I know what you are thinking, customers don't understand IT (from a detailed technical perspective), they look to us to provide services that they don't even know exist or have no idea how to get, so it's up to us to decide for them and/or just tell them what they need. You are correct. Customers don't know, nor should they, the technical aspects IT provides, but bear with me for a few minutes as I explain what I mean.

Customers simply know that they want an outcome, and they need IT services and products to achieve it. However, they don't really care about how they reach the outcome they want, as long as it is provided quickly, reliably, and meets their budget. They absolutely don't care about all the details IT must go through to provide the service or product. Following our previous pizza example, if you are ordering a pizza, do you really care about what kind of oven they use, the order of ingredients added to the pizza before cooking, how they fold the delivery box, the type of delivery car or the route that the delivery driver takes to get to you? You get my point. Most if not all of these details, while extremely relevant to the pizza company/delivery driver are irrelevant to you as the customer. You just care that you get the pizza, it is of good quality, price, and delivered at the time that you expected.

As times change, so do the expectations of the customer, you must understand what they do and why in order to truly understand how to provide value with the products and services in IT. So, how do you meet customer expectations? In the end, speaking to the customer and establishing what they want, or need is really the only way to do this. For example, when starting a new contract, I meet with all the key stakeholders and discuss contractual requirements with them, before asking, "if this project was a success and fully met your expectations, 30-60-90 days, 6-months, 1 year, 5 years, 10 years down the road, what does that look like to you?" It never surprises me that their answer is not 100% aligned with the requirements spelled in the contract. It is not that they are substantially different or need to change them, it's just that being clear in a Request for Proposal (RFP) in writing is much more difficult than it sounds, or the key stakeholder may not have been involved in writing the RFP themselves.

Eliciting customer expectations

There are many ways to elicit customer expectations. All of which require a critical understanding of the customer, what they want and what they need. In the past, it may have been easy for IT to anticipate a service or product by assuming the customer's desire - after all, we are consumers of IT as well. We know what we want and therefore, our wants should also scale to customer desires to some degree or another. I was at a conference recently and heard a reputable IT leader say something along the lines of "Apple® never talks to their customers to understand what they want. They just know. Then they go and create something new that everyone loves." I can't speak for Apple, but my guess is that the statement is not wholly accurate. Yes, Apple have done a fantastic job of creating new and life-changing products and services, no doubt. While I do agree they keep new technologies under close guard, I would venture a guess in saying that they do not create anything in a vacuum. How they determine what a customer wants is part of their "secret sauce." Whether they are researching, talking to customers or hiring/allowing employees to solve problems that they experience themselves as customers, they are in lock-step with understanding what customers really want.

Clarifying Questions

Asking for clarification in the customer's own words is a great way of understanding their perspective of what success looks like. As I described earlier, every person has their own notions of success or value, so it should be understood from each key stakeholders' point of view. For example, I work for a contractor to the U.S. Federal Government. When we bid on a new contract, the government provides us a very detailed list of activities and expectations in the form of a request for proposal (RFP). We go through the RFP and address all of the requirements as they are spelled out. Upon being awarded a contract, we have two choices. One, take everything in the contract as the *only* expectations the customer wants, after all, they were very clear in the RFP. Success, right? The real answer is sometimes, but not always. The second choice we have is to understand what everyone's expectations actually are and then add that to the contractual requirements. Throughout my career, I have found that the contract in comparison to customer expectations are rarely 100% the same. Sure, the contract clearly outlines the criteria that needs to be met, and if that's all we provided, we would meet the contractual obligations, but we would not make the customers 100% happy.

Asking questions helps you understand what each stakeholder's outcome must look like to ensure a successful outcome. Once you understand these, even if you can't meet them entirely, you can better manage their expectations and their perceptions of the value you are providing. Increasing the perception of value is the key to customer happiness. Whatever you do, however you do it, if you put the customer's real wants and needs at the center of your approach, your chances of success increase.

Five Whys

Asking "why" five times is a critical step in knowing what your customer wants. What they perceive as valuable. You can start off by asking "what is it you're looking for?". To illustrate, when discussing a specific service-level agreement (SLA), the customer may respond with something along the lines of "it's important to meet this SLA because it's what we promised our customer, users, and/or departments." You should take that information, and ask "why is it important to your customers, users and/or departments that you meet this SLA?" Whatever their answer, you should ask "and why is that important and so on until you get to the root of the expectations.

Additionally, after you receive the answers, you need to relay it back to make sure you have accurately recorded their points: this also gives you another chance to dig deeper into their expectations. You should keep the dialog going until you fully understand what it is that they're trying to do, why they're trying to do it, and how your services fit into meeting those expectations.

Note, when using the Five Whys methods, it is critical that you let the customer know that you understand the importance of meeting the requirements (e.g. contractual, SLA, etc.) and that you will, but you really need to get to the reason the requirement exists in the first place. After all, if the requirement is just there because it is something they have always done and measured rather than leading to increased value for their customers, users or departments, it may just be another number that no one really looks at. Even though this is called The Five Why's, it may actually be more or fewer times. It is just a thought process to help get to the real reasons and understand what they value.

Customer Experience (CX)

In a recent report, it was found that CX will be (or in many cases already is) the number one reason customers choose to do or not do business with a company.

While historically, IT seemed to have been (somewhat) immune to certain customer experience and satisfaction requirements with the success of technologies such as cloud (e.g. Infrastructure as a Service – IaaS, Platform as a Service – PaaS and Software as a Service – SaaS), this is no longer the case. Customers today, including internal ones, have more choice than ever and are more than willing to exercising that.

You have no doubt heard the term CX recently. What is CX? It is all about the customer's interactions with your organization and how they perceive them. The Customer Experience Professionals Association™ (CXPA.org) identifies six core competencies for CX.

1. Customer-Centric Culture
2. Voice of the Customer, Customer Insight, and Understanding
3. Organizational Adoption and Accountability
4. Customer Experience Strategy
5. Experience Design, Improvement, and Innovation
6. Metrics, Measurement, and ROI

At first glance, these core topics look a lot like the aspects we have already been measuring, managing and delivering for decades, however, after digging deeper into each one a bit more, it is clear that there is room for growth and improvement.

Customer-Centric Culture

Culture is at the core of CX. It's the way we (as an organization) behave regardless of whether anyone is looking or not. Every organization is different in this regard. If the focus is on IT from technology alone, we will miss the overarching reason for our existence; to provide products and services that meet customer standards.

Creating a customer-centric culture requires an organizational mindset change where the customer comes first, they are the reason for everything that we do after all. CX is about understanding your customers and then building offerings to meet their needs, wants and desires. To be truly successful, your services must provide value as perceived by the customer.

As I described earlier, the value is whatever a customer perceives it to be. If they perceive it to be of good value, then it is good. If they perceive it to be of bad value, then it is bad. If you want happy customers, you must know them, their wants, needs and desires. Then build, deliver and improve everything you do around meeting these understandings to provide the best value. As Peter Drucker said, "quality in a product or service is not what the supplier puts in. It is what the customer gets out and is willing to pay for."

There are many ways to begin to understand your customer and build a customer-centric culture. According to Annette Franz (CX-Journey.com), "your organizational purpose and core values must align with the customer values". I often say, if you don't know where you are going, you will get there. When you arrive, you may not like it, but you will arrive anyway. So, if you want to have a customer-centric culture, you must know the "where" and the "why" and those must align with what your customers want.

Voice of the customer (VoC), Customer Insight and Understanding

VoC is the process of monitoring, collecting, analyzing, and reporting on all customer feedback channels to understand customer interaction with an organization. There are many tools of measurement identified for VoC, including: Customer Effort Score (CES) – how easy it is to do business with your organization, Net Promoter Score (NPS) – how likely they are to recommend you to someone, Customer Satisfaction (CSAT) – how satisfied they are with an interaction, product or service, Customer Lifetime Value (CLV) – the overall profitability of the customer over time and many more.

VoC requires more than simple customer satisfaction surveys, which, while providing insight into customer perception, lack validity because of leading questions. For example, have you ever seen an organization's customer satisfaction survey scores consistently rating as very satisfied, but when you talk to the customers, they say they "hate IT" or "IT never works?" - why is this?

Where is the disconnect? It is in the questions we are asking. If we write questions that are simply surveying the technician that provided the service rather than the ability to meet the customer's expectation and overall business needs, these discrepancies will continue to occur.

The key takeaway is that to understand your customer, you must truly find what they want from you and why, and how they perceive what you are providing for them before determining what to do with that data. This is to not only keep customers but improve their experiences so that they sing your praises from the mountain top to everyone they come in contact with.

Organizational Adoption and Accountability

Adoption and Accountability are all about ensuring business goals are aligned with a customer-centric model. As with other governance programs, knowing who is accountable for what, where, when and how is critical to success. Are your C-Level leaders engaged and committed to a customer-centric culture? Without the executive leadership's buy-in and commitment, the success of any program is low.

The key takeaway is, organizational leadership must be on-board and in alignment with your CX plans, all staff must be accountable and empowered to facilitate their initiatives, and company policies must be in place to drive the organization's ongoing success.

Customer Experience Strategy

IT is very familiar with strategy processes in general, including the CX strategy that helps to define, design and deliver plans and outcomes. We must define the experience, develop the processes and behaviors, communicate the plan and engage and empower employees to ensure CX success.

There are many steps and methods that will assist you in creating a successful CX strategy, from defining a vision, defining customer personas (a generic, high level, fictional overview of a specific customer that defines who they are, what they do, how they interact with your product or service, etc.), ensuring executive commitment, and defining all the steps, people, processes and tools required for success.

The key point is that strategy is all about planning and defining the desired outcomes, directions, commitments, communications, people, and tools required to meet your CX effort.

Employee Engagement

As part of CX, we must not forget our people. Once we know what a customer wants and how we are going to deliver it to them, it is critical to ensure your employees are moving towards the same target in order to establish the success of the program. This focus on the employee is very similar to the VoC program's methods and processes, the goal being to understand your employees, what makes them tick, and how to engage them. If they are not engaged, they may not be meet your customer's expectations. This is a symbiotic relationship.

Employee engagement (EE) is more than just checking in with the employees and doing satisfaction surveys, or planning activities, games, and events. It is the culture of your organization. Fundamentally, EE is understanding and increasing the value each employee perceives they are receiving from their employment with the organization. It is the understanding and measurement of how passionate they are about their job and the organization. This is derived from questions you must ask such as, do they know why they are there, what their roles are, and what success they bring to the organization. Just like with value from a customer perspective, if an employee perceives value as poor, it's poor. If it's good, its good.

Experience Design, Improvement, and Innovation

Design, Improvement and Innovation are nothing new to us in IT, we design new products, services, and programs on a daily basis. We constantly improve everything, and we look for innovations at all levels. Creating a successful CX is also very similar, we must understand the outcomes, requirements and associated changes.

Additionally, we should use more strategic methods like Design Thinking when engaging customers and employees. A cognitive, strategic and practical process used in design that are facilitated through a hands-on, user-centric approach to problem-solving. Because Design Thinking is human-centric, using the five-step process of Empathize, Define, Ideate, Prototype, and Test, can lead to innovation and eventually better customer experiences.

The key note to make is that we need to identify the interdependencies between people, process and design tools, follow well-designed processes and use design thinking to engage both customers *and* employees.

Metrics, Measurement, and ROI

Metrics are critically important to any initiative. As we say, what gets measured, gets done. It helps us align our people, process and tools with the specific outcomes that meet the customer's idea of value. However, just because you can measure something, doesn't necessarily mean that it needs to be measured and reported to customers. There are internal and external measurements, metrics and reports that you may use.

The key takeaway is that the ROI (Return on Investment) must make sense and anything you measure and report, internally or externally, need to be in support of the customer's expectation of increasing value.

Customer Journey mapping

Simply stated, journey mapping is a graphical representation of all the interactions (also known as touchpoints) a customer has with your organization, service or product and how they feel about said touch points. There are many tools and templates you can find online or in books to help you with your journey mapping exercise. Before you begin, you need to know what journey you are going to be mapping, who is taking the journey, and who is responsible, accountable, consulted, informed and/or influences said journey.

There are four general steps to creating a journey map:

1. Conduct initial interviews – In speaking with customers and stakeholders, you can determine all of the steps and how they feel about each. The goal is to record their statements about the products, services, and interactions with your organization from their perspective. Try not to be defensive, rather, just matter of fact. The more open they are with you, the better the opportunity you have to ensure the journey meets their expectations and provides value.

2. Determine the details of each touchpoint – Once you understand what all the touchpoints are along a specific journey, you need to understand the customer and stakeholders' perceptions of each. How do they view the interaction? How do they feel about it? What would they change if they could and why? The more you can dig into their views, the easier it will be to address any concerns.

3. Compile all data onto a map (see example in Figure 9) – After the interviews, you should have a pretty clear understanding of what all the touchpoints are and how your customers feel about the interactions. Compiling this data onto a journey map is the next step. Again, there are many tools, templates and applications available to you for creating journey maps.

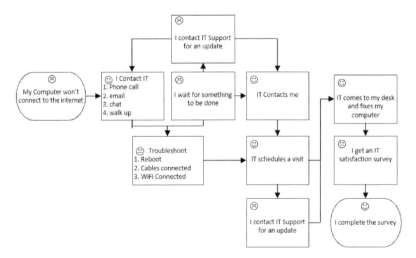

Figure 9: Example Journey Map

There is no singular right method or mapping technique either. The goal is to take the interview and touchpoint data you collected and create a graphical representation of the journey to understand how the customers feel about each step along the way. This also identifies areas of concern, needs for improvement and what you're doing very well.

4.   Address the results and recommendations - The fourth step is to study your map to determine what it all means. Are you doing everything right? Are there areas you thought you were doing well in, but after the journey mapping exercise found otherwise? What do you need to do to achieve the outcomes you desire? These are just a few questions to consider. The goal with results and recommendations is to create a very short list of 3 to 5 items that, if you focused on, would make the biggest difference in providing value to your customer. This list then becomes your recommendation for change/implementation.

Value stream mapping

One final area I would like to add to your arsenal before we leave this chapter is Value Stream Mapping (VSM). VSM is a Lean technique used for documenting, analyzing and improving the flow of anything required in producing or delivering products or services for a customer. This is much like customer journey mapping but specifically for the internal processes we utilize in IT.

The goal of VSM, like Lean itself, is to identify, reduce or eliminate waste and ensure the flow is constant and uninterrupted. Also, like the Customer Journey Map, there are no shortages of ideas about what should be included or how it should be created. In short, VSM graphically depicts the step by step movements across the flow of items as they progress through a process, allowing you to easily see where waste is occurring, so you can correct the issues. Additionally, VSM provides measurements, metrics, problem identification and improvement plans for the process itself.

You may ask, if the outcome already meets the customer's expectations, why is it important to eliminate or reduce waste during the flow? There are many nuances to the answer here, but suffice to say, if something is as waste-free and uninterrupted as possible, it stands to reason that we can then deliver better *AND* faster *AND* cheaper. This results in happier customers who perceive a higher value of the products and services you are providing.

Key Takeaways

- IT's job is to provide value, not technologies. Value is whatever the customer perceives it to be.
- What's amazing today will be expected tomorrow. You always need to look to the future to keep wowing customers.
- Meeting SLA and/or contractual requirements does not necessarily mean meeting customer expectations.
- First, understand who your customers are and what they value, then determine what is needed to facilitate the outcomes customers want.
- Understanding your customer, their wants and desires, are required for success. Meet with your customers and ask questions. Get to the root of why they want, need and expect something and your chances for success increase.
- CX is the key differentiator. A customer-centric culture is the only way to meet expectations and set your organization apart.
- Engaged Employees are critical to an organization's success.
- Utilize tools such as Customer Journey and Value Stream maps to understand your customer, your employees, and your processes.

CHAPTER 3:

ISM FRAMEWORKS, MODELS, AND PROCESSES

Frameworks here, frameworks there, frameworks everywhere! We love our Frameworks in IT, the more the merrier. Since IT is made of people who solve logical problems for a living, and we relentlessly receive pressure to do more with fewer resources, reliably and of higher quality at cheaper costs (you get the picture), it only makes sense that we look for repeatable methods to define, standardize and streamline the things we create, deliver and support. For the purposes of this chapter, I will refer to frameworks, business models and processes as simply frameworks.

It is important to understand that the inception, growth, and maturity of each of these frameworks come from the way that IT itself has developed as an iterative and creative process. As IT grew, different ideas of how specific functions should be handled also increased. Additionally, as IT matured, groups (intentional or inadvertently) developed silos between them (see chapter 1). All moving to the same end goal, but rarely working with each other in the same way. Therefore, while not the initial intent, it makes sense that there is not one specific process or standard that suits all of the needs.

Because IT evolved into a silo-based structure over time, different groups have identified frameworks that would solve one or multiple problems for them or their customer, rather than IT as a whole. From their team's perspective, selection of a framework was easy, because it best fit their need. After selection, they would push forward with adoption regardless of what other IT groups' thoughts, needs or outcomes were.

They would also defend the framework to the end, claiming it be the one that would solve all of IT's problems. It worked for their team, so others should just know the benefit and adopt the framework too.

Because, IT is very wide in scope and every group, while aiming for the same goal, have different means of getting there, many frameworks have been created, adopted and adapted over time.

I am not under the illusion that no matter which frameworks I discuss here, I will miss some that you may have heard of or use in your own organization. Lists of frameworks in IT seem nearly endless and each is designed for very specific purposes to solve problems and implement a standard way of doing something. My intention of this chapter is to give you an overall understanding of what I consider the most important frameworks of today, what they do, how they work together and how integrating them will not only solve certain technical issues, but realign the teams to a customer-centric model and reduce the duplication of effort (and IT spend).

In this chapter, we will discuss ITIL, LeanIT, Agile, DevOps and Organizational Change Management. Together these make up the core frameworks of ISM. I will give a brief overview of what each of them does, as well as how they can work together to provide an end-to-end IT Service Management approach. Until recently these frameworks appeared to be in direct conflict with each other, but this is not the case. ISM ensures value to the customer and meets the current and future challenges – *better AND faster AND cheaper.*

ITIL

ITIL was developed in the 1980s by the British Government to address service quality. Since its inception, it has grown and undergone several iterations in its overall maturity. ITIL is a non-prescriptive, end-to-end, lifecycle approach to service management and defines the structure of IT through a set of practices that help IT design and delivery services provide value to the business. ITIL has evolved since its first inception and currently in a 4th revision. ITIL v4 defines the processes and language around seven guiding principles:

1. Focus on value
2. Design for experience

3. Start where you are

4. Work holistically

5. Progress iteratively

6. Observe directly

7. Be transparent

It adopts and adapts a holistic approach to IT products and services, and lays out the entire lifecycle, stages, and processes involved to ensure success and value to customers. The current ITIL v4 certification scheme was developed by Axelos and is detailed in Figure 10.

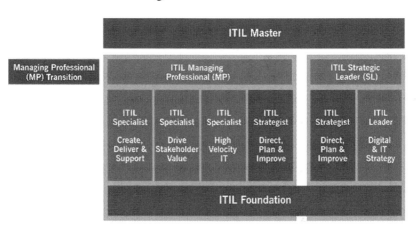

Figure 10: ITIL 4 certification scheme - by AXELOS. Copyright © AXELOS Limited 2018. All rights reserved. Material is reproduced under license from AXELOS Limited.

Historically, ITIL adoption and adaptation projects have been a very large undertaking for IT. Unfortunately, in a lot of cases, these projects were never finished or reached the expected outcome. It should be noted that this level of failure was and still is normal (although not acceptable), the failure rate outcome for any project is between 14% and 33% according to PMI.

Additionally, the term "non-prescriptive" has been historically misunderstood to a large degree. Practitioners adopted an understanding that non-prescriptive meant following the approach as described to the dot, otherwise not using it at all.

Further to this, it pushes to adopt and adapt all aspects of ITIL without truly understanding the scope, including providing adequate resources and funding, and gaining the appropriate leadership buy-in and commitment. For example, I am often asked to help an organization "adopt and adapt ITIL." Every time I ask the same three questions. "What part of ITIL, what's your timeframe and what is your budget?" Almost always the answer is "All of ITIL, 90 days and we really don't have a specific budget." I am oversimplifying here, but you get the picture.

These misunderstandings have also led to a lot of undeserved negativity about ITIL across IT over time. Suffice to say, ITIL is a very large framework and when understood, adopted and adapted correctly, successfully sets the stage for all other ISM approaches.

LeanIT

An extension of Lean Manufacturing principles (derived mostly from the Toyota Production System), LeanIT is an improvement methodology that is focused on reducing or eliminating waste in an attempt to provide value to the development and management of IT products and services.

LeanIT identifies three areas of waste:

1. Muda - pure waste, such as defects, rework, over processing and overproduction
2. Muri – overburdening of resources
3. Mura – variability in delivery

Elimination of waste (Muda) is the primary goal of LeanIT, making things better *AND* faster *AND* cheaper.

Waste is anything that is not done right the first time, to the standard that is requested. IT often over-think and overproduce with the mentality that it helps to provide more value. For example, our processes are very specific. We work hard to develop them and after they are in place, work even harder to make them more specific. In some cases, we may take this too far, resulting in an actual reversal of outcomes.

Overburdening of resources (Muri) is often a failure point for IT, and not having enough to do a specific job can cause burnout. Sometimes we plan for a specific amount of resources to be available for a project rollout, and as it turns out, we have overestimated the amount necessary, or worse yet, there are not enough to provide the required support. This ambiguity coupled with the customer's desire to constantly reduce the cost often leads to us giving more tasks to staff members and not backfilling when people leave.

In addition, ensuring an even flow of delivery (Mura) is a key concept of LeanIT. The concept promotes reducing or eliminating via Just-In-Time processes, and uses "pull" based systems to ensure that only what is needed is delivered upon request at any given point. For example, if you were building computers on an assembly line and your job was to install hard drives, you would ask (pull system) for a hard drive when you were ready to install it, rather than having a pile of hard drives waiting (push system) for a new order to be processed. The goal is to only have what you need when you need it, otherwise, it is excessive and a waste that needs to be limited or eliminated altogether.

Agile

Agile is a mindset applied to a group of frameworks designed to streamline processes and produce high-value output for customers. A small group of developers got together in 2001 and created the Agile Manifesto (see - http://agilemanifesto.org/), a set of twelve principles for uncovering better ways of developing software, guided by four core values:

- *Individuals and Interactions over processes and tools*
- *Working Software over comprehensive documentation*
- *Customer Collaboration over contract negotiation*
- *Responding to Change over following a plan*

There are many ideas and terms involved with Agile, all designed for a specific outcome. For the purposes of this book however, I will only cover a couple of the main concepts of Agile.

Project Management

From a project perspective, Agile is designed to adapt to changes quickly, work with customers often, and deliver excellent value for money. Agile breaks work into small increments and iterations called sprints, to deliver outcomes in short time frames (timeboxes).

Agile project teams are made up of staff from across all areas of IT. This cross-functional team is critical to outcomes being more diverse, and therefore more stable.

Agile's product backlog is simply a prioritized list of all the desired items to be added to a product or service. The backlog is derived from conversations and/or requests from customers.

Visual Management

Kanban is a scheduling system developed by Taiichi Ohno, from Toyota, to improve manufacturing efficiency. The visual representation is done using a Kanban board. Kanban boards illustrate where the steps, statuses, and roadblocks (delays) in providing an even flow exist. The Kanban board (see example Figure 11) is broken into sections or work efforts that encompass a specific process in an overall work effort cycle. It starts with the backlog and ends with completed items, while every step in between is completely up to the project requirements. The thing to understand is that how it looks is completely up to you. Each process has a work in progress (WIP) limit, which is the maximum limit of how many things a specific stage can be working on at a time. In the example depicted in Figure 11, WIP for process 4 is 2. There are already 2 items in progress at that stage. Nothing from the previous stage can proceed to the next one, even if it is ready to. It has to wait until one of the 2 items already in WIP moves to complete, thus freeing up a WIP slot.

Backlog	Selected WIP = 3	Process 1 WIP = 6	Process 2 WIP = 3	Process 3 WIP = 7	Process 4 WIP = 2	Complete

Figure 11: Kanban Board Example

This wait time to move from one step to the next is considered waste. The goal is to keep the flow moving evenly. Kanban boards are a great visual tool that shows where things are not flowing efficiently so that we can adjust the proper resources, settings, etc. to eliminate the backlog.

DevOps

DevOps has received enormous acceptance and traction in the IT community lately, and rightfully so. It is defined as a cross between Development and Operations, and more than just a new term or buzzword. DevOps is a philosophy, a movement from practitioners by practitioners, that helps build a collaborative culture inside and across all of IT. DevOps is built on ITIL, Agile and Lean and works to automate development activities to provide software faster and more reliably.

DevOps began as a grassroots movement derived from Patrick DuBois' desire to understand IT, and his frustrations as he recognized the chasm between the Development and Operations teams. Over time Patrick and other practitioners came together at different events to discuss, create and mature, what we now know today as DevOps.

Three Ways

Gene Kim introduced the concept of Three Ways in his book *The Phoenix Project: A Novel About IT, DevOps, and Helping Your Business Win*. From the Three Ways, all other DevOps can be derived.

Figure 12: First Way: Adapted from Gene Kim, 'The Three Ways: The Principles Underpinning DevOps"

First Way (Flow – Left to Right -Figure 12). Flow is all about providing value quickly and efficiently between Development and Operations. The goal is to reduce and optimize time for deployments while increasing reliability and quality. This is accomplished by adopting and adapting ITIL, Agile and Lean principles of increased visibility, reducing waste, and continuously improving and optimizing processes.

Figure 13: Second Way: Adapted from Gene Kim, 'The Three Ways: The Principles Underpinning DevOps"

Second Way (Feedback – Right to Left -Figure 13). Feedback is paramount to the maturity of any organization. Fast, continual and reciprocal feedback between Development and Operations at all levels is critical to creating safer, more resilient work systems.

Figure 14: Third Way: Adapted from Gene Kim, 'The Three Ways: The Principles Underpinning DevOps"

Third Way (Continual Learning and Experimentation -Figure 14). All about building a specific culture of continual learning and experimentation in the organization. At its core it is about breaking down silos between support organizations, reducing fear and increasing trust.

Successful DevOps

For DevOps to be fully successful it is important to understand that you must take a holistic view of services from end-to-end. You need a customer-centric culture that champions the collaboration and breaks down silos between support groups to increase value for the customer. Next, you need to look at your processes and integrate ITIL, LeanIT, and Agile to improve flow. Finally, automation across tools and the toolchain is needed to increase the speed of delivery, flexibility, and stability.

Organizational Change Management

Organizational Change Management (OCM) is the management of change from a people's perspective, specifically regarding the readiness of the organization in making that change. It should not be confused with Technical Change Management, which focuses on the tactical-technical alterations itself.

OCM includes both the organizational structure as well as the culture, from reporting why people do what they do, to communication, change readiness and ensuring sustained change.

OCM is arguably the most overlooked part of change across all areas of the organization, which is a shame as when aspects of OCM are taken into consideration early on, championed by leadership, and embedded in the culture of the organization, the success of changes are much higher and longer lasting.

Change is difficult because it not only includes the technical steps and integrations, but the people, and how they feel . Managing these feelings can establish how ready the people are and highlight any resistance. If people are not engaged, the change will either be slow to succeed or fail entirely. People are at the center of all successful changes. Can you remember a time where a change was thrust upon you and you resisted? Or a time where you were making the change and even though it made total sense to you, people still resisted? Of course, you have, we all have. To ensure success, we must engage our people, early and often, and to engage them, we must understand a few basic psychology truths regarding motivation, individual differences, learning theory, and change models.

Change Curve

First introduced by Swiss-American psychiatrist Elisabeth Kübler-Ross in her 1969 book *On Death and Dying*, the Change Curve (see Figure 15) identifies seven key stages that individuals go through during a loss, letting go of the past and engaging with a different future. In this context, death, loss, and change are viewed by our brains as the same concept.

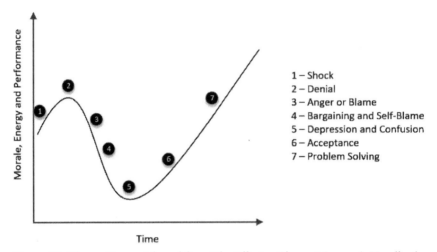

Figure 15: Change Curve. Adapted from The Effective Change Manager's Handbook

It is extremely important to understand that everyone goes through some, if not all of these tasks, for a change. Also, while some tasks may be navigated in a different order than shown in Figure 15 or even skipped entirely, it takes different amounts of time for each person to progress through them. Some people move quickly, while others move slower. Some people are at ease with change while others are not. If we understand this, then we can plan for and communicate changes in advance to help succeed in implanting them smoothly and permanently.

While people handle and accept change differently, without effective planning, everyone will enter the process abruptly, and you will most likely end up fighting while trying to implement the tactical change itself. This increases the effort, resistance and potential for failure. Effective planning will curb the overall negative impact and increase your chances of successful change, so start the people engagement as early as you can.

Business Relationship Management

Business Relationship Management (BRM) is the function of understanding and facilitating all aspects of relationships between the company and the service provider. It is the connector between these groups and their sub-groups to help all sides win. The heart of BRM is built on the best practices of Customer Relationship Management (CRM) but is expanded from the organization's external customers to include internal ones as well.

From an ITSM perspective, BRM has been around since the begging. According to the BRM Institute®, it "gained legitimacy in 2005 with ISO/ IEC 20000 service management standard and was reinforced with the release of ITIL v3 in 2007" (The BRMP® Guide to the BRM Body of Knowledge).

Connector, Orchestrator, and Navigator

BRM encompasses all the knowledge, skills and behaviors that drive win-win relationships between all parties and the application of these areas to ensure successful outcomes and value. BRM can be a function, role, and capability all at the same time. It is more art than science and requires empathy, communication skills, and the ability to know when and how to use influence to guide winning relationships.

BRMs are the customer's advocate, ensuring the VoC is heard, understood, and integrated into the strategy and design of services by the service provider. They are also the voice of delivery, ensuring capabilities, readiness and ability to meet the customer's demands are understood and accounted for prior to any agreements being made. This means BRMs sometimes works 51% for the customer and 49% for the provider of the service or vice versa. This occasionally puts the BRM professional (BRMP) in precarious positions. As Abraham Lincoln said when quoting John Lydgate's poem "You can please some of the people all of the time, you can please all of the people some of the time, but you can't please all the people all of the time"

BRM is made up of three main components:

1. *Governance:* Protects BRM as a key aspect of provider capability.
2. *Core BRM Disciplines:* Demand Shaping, Exploring, Servicing and Value Harvesting.
3. *BRM Competencies:* Supports the BRM role and ensures it has the *competencies* to be effective in delivering value to both the provider organization and its business partners. Includes Strategic partnering, Business IQ, Portfolio Management, Provider Domain, Powerful Communications, and Business Transition Management.

Integrated Service Management

Organizations are changing and demanding better, faster, and cheaper services from IT. The only way to provide all three is to integrate the existing frameworks the organization is already utilizing according to their specific strengths. For example, ITIL is at the core of all the ISM frameworks and provides the structure and central language for all other processes to succeed. LeanIT provides the best processes for continual improvement. Agile enables fast deployments and project management. DevOps engages all teams cross-national and automates provisioning across the lifecycle. OCM ensures individual, organization, communication and change engagement. It is critical to understand that ALL of these are important and no one framework alone is more significant than the other, nor can they be fully successful on their own in a vacuum or silo. All of them have their individual strengths, but need to complement each other for the organization's success.

Approaching frameworks as complementary instead of standalone also helps with conflicting agendas and budgetary clashes. For example, if an IT Development team think that an IT Operations team is going to take their budget to do the same thing they are trying to do, they will push back, however, if they work in conjunction with other teams, focusing on their framework's strength, conflicting budgetary priorities diminish or disappear entirely.

ISM was developed by Pink Elephant and Professional Designations to address how ITIL, LeanIT, Agile, DevOps, and Organizational Change Management practices collectively enable process acceleration, increase efficiency, lower costs and deliver business value. Figure 16 highlights the ISM integrations, detailing the steps for which group does what, and encompasses the entirety of an IT department's delivery operations (i.e. IT Operations and IT Development).

Basically, ISM brings together all the best parts of each framework. Separately, each of these frameworks do a great job at a set of very specific practices, however when separate, they continue to work in silos and compete with each other for methodology, control and budget. Together, they use the best of each framework to deliver IT products and services to customers better *AND* faster *AND* cheaper.

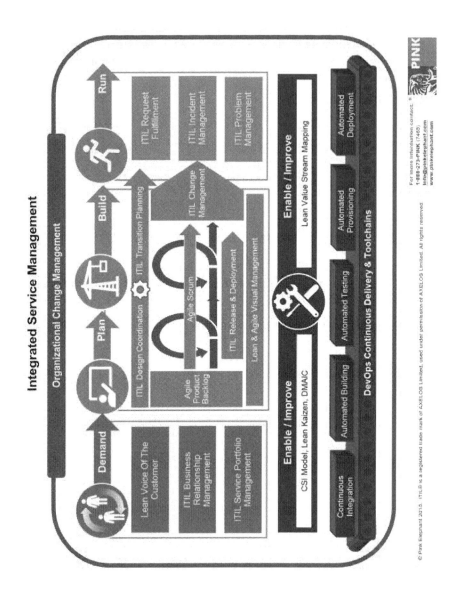

Figure 16: Integrated Service Management - Image reproduced with permission from PinkElephant

Key Takeaways

- The biggest challenge facing IT is the need to provide services to customer better, AND faster AND cheaper.

- ITIL is at the core of ISM and will continue to be a major part of the strategic response to new challenges and ways of working in IT.

- ISM helps reduce silo-based conflicting agendas, budgetary clashes, and duplication efforts, resulting in increased customer value and satisfaction.

- ISM uses and realigns the strengths of existing groups, tools, technologies, frameworks and models to facilitate value through a customer-centric culture.

- As support organizations continually face increased mandates to consolidate and economize IT services, success requires leveraging cross-trained resources to optimize existing tools and technologies.

- Flattening the organization to deliver greater value to the customer requires commitment from the top management to drive an organizational culture change from a focus on IT to one of the customers.

- It is essential to move solutions closer to the customer, creating a more positive support experience and meeting their expectations of receiving immediate responses.

- There is no one model that will do or be it all. Integrated Service Management (ITIL, Lean, Agile, DevOps, and Organizational Change Management) frameworks, build on and are complementary to each other, providing a collaborative approach to technical service and support for both now and the future.

CHAPTER 4:

ITSM FRAMEWORKS, STANDARDS, AND BEST PRACTICES

There are as many ITSM frameworks, standards, models and best practices (FSMBP) as there are business needs themselves. Having an environment in which we can pick and choose a specific FSMBP that suits the needs of IT is both a strength and a weakness. Having separate FSMBP's allows IT to target areas of weaknesses and find a solution. However, because there are many options, it is hard to choose any single, best, definitive FSMBP for all IT groups to operate under. This has led to increased lines of demarcation between IT support teams and in some cases a culture of competition between the groups.

Like with ISM frameworks described in the previous chapter, I understand that no matter which FSMBP I list or discuss here, I will miss some that you may have heard of or use in your organization. My intention for this chapter is to give you an overall understanding of a few key FSMBPs that I have found helpful in ensuring an end-to-end view of ITSM service and support.

In this chapter we will discuss CMMI, COBIT, HDI, ISO, NIST, and PMI. In summary:

- CMMI – Ensures the maturity of a company's process and ability to deliver on promised work.
- COBIT – Helps increase trust in and value from IT. Is used by many leading audit organizations and helps ensure governance.
- HDI – Helps increase technician enthusiasm, defines best practices for service and supports and increases customer satisfaction.
- ISO/IEC – Provides guidance for and helps improve business processes to reduce waste and cost.

- NIST – Defines the Information Security program and covers five core areas (Identify, Protect, Detect, Respond, and Recover).
- PMI – Helps ensure projects create and sustain value.

All these FSMBP work together in support of ISM. I will give a brief overview of what each of them is, as well as how they can work symbiotically to provide the overall governance, culture of innovation, and structure of successful end-to-end ITSM.

CMMI

Capability Maturity Model Integration (CMMI) manages processes and integrating activities across an organization. Originating in software development, CMMI was established at Carnegie Mellon University as a process level improvement training and appraisal program.

The CMMI model is a proven set of the best global practices that enable organizations to build and benchmark their key capabilities.

The goal of CMMI is to define, build and mature an organization's capabilities to reduce risk, increase productivity, improve business performance and increase customer satisfaction. It is measured using five distinct maturity levels of CMMI:

0. Incomplete
1. Initial
2. Managed
3. Defined
4. Quantitatively Managed
5. Optimizing

The maturity levels are identified through a formal appraisal process and help organizations demonstrate their reliability of process to customers and business partners.

COBIT

Control Objectives for Information and Related Technologies (COBIT) is a framework developed by ISACA for the lifecycle of governance, strategy, and tactical management within the IT domain. COBIT provides a comprehensive process that defines the components to build and sustain a governance system including processes, organizational structures, policies and procedures, information flows, culture and behaviors, skills, and infrastructure.

COBIT separates governance and management objectives. Governance ensures a balance between the stakeholder and organization, logical direction, and agreed performance, and measurements are monitored. Management plans, builds, runs and monitors activities to meet enterprise objectives.

Together there are 40 governance and management objectives defined in COBIT. Governance objectives are grouped in the COBIT Evaluate, Direct and Monitor (EDM) domain and Management objectives are grouped into four others: Align, Plan and Organize (APO), Build, Acquire and Implement (BAI), Deliver, Service and Support (DSS) and Monitor, Evaluate and Assess (MEA).

HDI

HDI (thinkhdi.com) is a professional association and certification body for the technical service and support industry. HDI's goal is to transform service and support organizations and reimagine their approach to delivering exceptional service and value. HDI provides events, certification, training, consulting, community membership and industry resources, and produces renowned publications and research, training and certifying thousands of professionals each year.

HDI's strength comes in three specific areas - Standards, Community and Events.

1. *Standards.* HDI's standards cover customer interaction skills for all IT levels including customer service, support desk, desktop support, team

leaders, managers and directors. These standards identify the process, critical skills and support center strategies, and help practitioners understand and most importantly implement key concepts that result in improved customer interactions. The HDI standards are a great resource for all IT staff when building and running a customer-centric service and support operation.

2. *Community*. HDIs community of leaders and connection of practitioners is unmatched worldwide. HDI provides innovative content from experts around the globe, exclusive research, and strategies for all segments of the industry, whitepapers, and an active community of support and service management professionals to expand their knowledge and advance their careers.

3. *Events*. HDI hold several annual events focused on Support Services and Service Management. These events bring together thousands of practitioners to learn how to implement the latest trends and strategic thinking in support center and employee management, and emerging technology certification standards.

There are so many benefits that my organization and staff members have received from HDI training and events, ranging from increased enthusiasm and utilization of best practices, to reduced turnover and eventually increased customer satisfaction. Additionally, our customers see the benefits of our dedication to customer service through the utilization of HDI standards on a daily basis.

ISO

International Organization for Standardization (ISO) is an independent, non-governmental international organization with a membership of 162 national standard bodies. Since its inception in 1947, ISO has developed over 20,000 standards across pretty much every industry.

ISO families are a series of standards collected and numbered that define the fundamentals of a given standard. For example, ISO 9000 is the family and ISO 9001:2015 is a specific standard. There are several ISO family related standards that apply to ITSM and cover pretty much every aspect of control. For this chapter, I will focus on a few key standards.

ISO 9000

Describes the fundamental concepts and principles of quality management. This family includes subjects under the Quality management system such as - Requirements, Fundamentals and vocabulary (definitions) and Managing for the sustained success of an organization (continuous improvement).

ISO/IEC 20000

• Describes the requirements for the service management (SM) system. This family includes subjects such as Service management system requirements, Guidance on the application of service management systems, Service providers, Process assessment model, Concepts and terminology, Guidance on the relationship between ISO/IEC 20000 and service management frameworks: ITIL®

ISO/IEC 27000

Comprises of information security standards published jointly by the ISO and the International Electrotechnical Commission (IEC). It provides the best practice recommendations on information security management, risk management, and controls. Its scope is very large and includes 45 separate standards, so for the purpose of the discussion, I will list the three key standards:

- ISO/IEC 27000 — Information security management systems — Overview and vocabulary
- ISO/IEC 27001 — Information technology - Security Techniques - Information security management systems-Requirements.
- ISO/IEC 27002 - Information technology — Security techniques — Code of practice for information security controls

Suffice to say security is a major focus of IT and the ISO/IEC 27000 family has grown and kept pace with the ever-changing requirements of managing security.

ISO/IEC 38500

Describes the corporate governance of IT for the organization and is published jointly by the ISO and the IEC. It provides a framework for effective governance of IT to assist organizations' understanding and fulfillment of legal, regulatory, and ethical obligations.

NIST

National Institute of Standards and Technology (NIST) was founded in 1901 and is now part of the U.S. Department of Commerce. NIST covers a wide range of standards, I will highlight NIST's cybersecurity framework (CSF).

In effect, NIST provides the What and the Why in the definition of a successful IT Security Program. NIST CSF consists of standards, guidelines, and best practices to manage cybersecurity-related risks. It is grouped into five concurrent and continuous functions:

1. Identify
2. Protect
3. Detect
4. Respond
5. Recover

In addition to the core framework, NIST Special Publication 800-series defines and reports on the Information Technology Laboratory's (ITL) research, guidelines, and outreach efforts in information system security, and on ITL's activity with industry, government, and academic organizations.

PMI

The Project Management Institute (PMI) provides globally recognized standards, certifications, resources, tools, academic research, publications, professional development courses, and networking opportunities. PMI has over 500,000 members in 208 countries, 300 chapters and enlists 10,000 volunteers in over 80 countries.

PMI has multiple credentials available for project and program managers. Their Project Management Professional (PMP)® certification has become a de facto standard certification in project management across all industries.

The PMP certification is based on the PMI Project Management Body of Knowledge (PMBOK) and encompasses five process groups and ten knowledge areas across the project lifecycle.

Process Groups:

1. Initiating
2. Planning
3. Executing
4. Monitoring and Controlling
5. Closing

Knowledge areas:

1. Project Integration Management
2. Project Scope Management
3. Project Schedule Management
4. Project Cost Management
5. Project Quality Management
6. Project Resource Management
7. Project Communications Management
8. Project Risk Management
9. Project Procurement Management
10. Project Stakeholder Management

Bringing it all together

While the guidance behind these Frameworks and FSDBPs is well thought out, vetted and documented, IT need to look at them as non-prescriptive in order to be effective. This means using what works best for the needs of the organization. People often get caught up in the mentality that everything is a "must do" when it comes to these FSDPBs. While I do agree that whatever you choose and implement needs to be done consistently in every aspect, ensuring that you use whatever makes sense to the extent that makes sense for your organization, is a critical part of understanding and using these SDBPs. I am not advocating following any or all of these blindly, just because someone created them and called them a best practice or standard. Rather, I am suggesting using what makes sense and then being consistent in your use.

With all these frameworks, models, standards and best practices, it easy to see why different groups lean heavier on one or two and why it can be confusing as to which one(s) should be used at all. Is ISO better than ITIL? Is PMI better than Agile? Or does DevOps work with IT Governance? So many options, how do we choose? Let's look a bit at how all of these FSDBPs work together.

There are eight specific areas in creating a successful, end-to-end ITSM program. Figure 17 highlights the Key Objectives mapped to the specific Frameworks, Standards, Models and Best Practices.

| Key Objective | Integrated Seervice Management™ | | | | | CMMI | COBIT | HDI | ISO 9000 | ISO/IEC 20000 | ISO/IEC 27000 | ISO/IEC 38500 | NIST | PMI |
	ITIL	LeanIT	Agile	DevOps	Org. Ch. Mgt.									
IT Governance	•						•					•		
IT Service Management	•									•				
IT Security	•			•							•		•	
IT Quality Management	•	•		•					•					
IT Project Management	•		•	•										•
IT Development	•	•	•	•	•									
IT Operations	•	•	•					•						
Culture of Innovation	•			•	•			•						

Figure 17: Key Objectives for ITSM Frameworks, Standards. Models and Best Practices

As you can see, there is some overlap on the list of eight key objectives. ITIL has some touchpoints in all of these Key Objective areas, but other standards and/or frameworks may also have touchpoints as well. This is one of the reasons for my previous statement, that we should use specific FSMBPs for specific needs, and in a non-prescriptive way. This will result in less overlap, but where it does it makes sense, some overlap will occur. In this specific case, ITIL is the language, so it will show in all areas, where for example NIST is really focused on security governance.

While it is interesting to see the overlap of key objectives in a table, I find it useful to view this from a house-based framework model as well. Figure 18 depicts the House of ITSM that aligns the relevant FSMBPs into an integrated, end-to-end whole. Each component of the Hours of ITSM includes a reference to the FSMBP associated with that specific area. For example, the roof of the House of ITSM is IT Governance and includes ITIL, COBIT and ISO/IEC 38500.

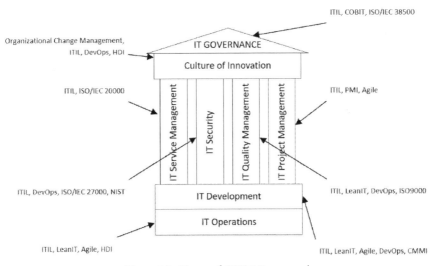

Figure 18: House of ITSM Framework.

In this model, IT Governance is the roof of the structure with IT Operations as the foundation, IT Development as the main floor and ITSM, Security, Quality and Project management as the pillars supporting the ceiling, which is the Culture of Innovation. All of these work in conjunction with eachother to enable all other areas of ITSM.

When you look at all of these together, you will see just how complementary they are to each other. If you use them for what they are best at, and not duplicate efforts across the models, your outcomes will be better *AND* faster *AND* cheaper, and your customers will be much happier with the delivery of your products and services.

Key Takeaways

- CMMI, COBIT, HDI, ISO, NIST, and PMI all work together in support of ISM.
- Taking a non-prescriptive approach to all ITSM FSMBP and using each for what it is best at will help you to eliminate or dramatically reduce duplication of effort.
- CMMI enables organizations to build and benchmark their key process capability maturity to customers and partners.
- COBIT helps organizations ensure compliance and governance in IT.
- HDI provides customer-centric standards, best practices, and skills training for the IT support and service industry.
- ISO defines the fundamentals and vocabulary for several standards utilized in IT.
- NIST provides a robust cybersecurity framework (CSF) that helps manage cybersecurity-related risks end-to-end.
- PMI provides the de facto standard certification in project management and best practices.

CHAPTER 5:

FUTURE OF ITSM

ITSM and IT are right on the cusp of one of the biggest changes ever seen. There are distinct pressures to improve the way IT works to provide increased value better *AND* faster *AND* cheaper due to developments like the focus on CX, the emergence of the cloud, artificial intelligence and automation, and competitive disruption activities worldwide.

Better *AND* faster *AND* cheaper. I often tell people, IT does a great job of the better and faster pieces. All the processes we have developed and matured over the years have helped IT get really good at the better and faster parts. It's the *cheaper* aspect that IT really seems to have problems with. Not because IT has unlimited budgets and can do anything it wants, but because it's the nature of IT to do things fast, which can result in a mistake, increased user issues, therefore requiring re-work and increased expenses.

IT always has time to fix things later, but rarely seems to have the time to do it right the first time. Time is really the primary focus from the customer's perspective. If something is broken, when do they want it fixed? Now! The question then is, how can you make things faster *AND* better *AND* cheaper at the same time?

The answer is to use what you already have, but in a way that allows you to reduce waste, produce higher quality and deliver faster services. How? The answer is ISM coupled with effective CX initiatives. IT needs to use the existing frameworks, standards, models and best practices in a more efficient manner. We need to break down the walls and silos between IT groups by rethinking what we do and why, and how we can move from a technology focus to a customer one. We need to ask ourselves the questions, does what I am doing, and how I am doing it, facilitate the outcome that the customer is seeking? If it is not, then why are we doing it?

Customer centricity is more than saying you are customer focused. It is truly believing and setting up an organizational culture that puts the customer's happiness at the center of everything you do. This is a holistic change for most organizations when you really look at the *WHY* of doing things. At the core, we all have restrictions, controls, and people (who all think and act differently) that determine what we do on a daily basis. If we can use these restrictions, controls and people's input as the details behind the HOW, and the customer's need as the WHY, then we can better design programs that meet customer requirements and expectations.

This holistic change in focus can be made by asking the question "What is it that you do?" This is a pretty basic question with what seems like would be a pretty basic answer, however, this is generally not the case. Each individual has their own unique answer. Additionally, when you really start listening, you realize that it doesn't really get to the real reason as to why the employees are there. Technicians at any level usually say I am here to provide X (where X is the name of their job title or the technology they work on). This misses the mark. Wouldn't a better response be, for example at an environmental conservancy company, IT technicians responding with something along the lines of "I save the planet." You could take the easy route and state that your job is the mission of your role, but does that really work well? Sometimes it does, however, that may not necessarily be the real objective. What if we have to answer this question in five words or less. That takes some thought, right? How can you answer this without knowing your customer? What do they want? How do they see things? If you put them first and ask, and then build your business around that, this question is a lot easier to answer. Again, you say, sure sounds good on paper, but I have a boss to answer to. You are correct, this change takes executive leadership buy-in and championing to actually work. If they don't think it's a good idea, the chances of the change becoming successfully implemented are much lower.

Innovation

In the 1960's Everett Rogers, an American communication theorist and sociologist described a natural rate of progression as the acceptance of new ideas. The acceptance timeline and market saturation can be classified into several groups, from innovators and early adopters to the majority and finally the laggards – see Figure 19. In the beginning, as with the emergence of any technology, there are innovators. These are the people/companies at the bleeding edge, accepting and adopting long ideas or technologies before everyone else. They not only lead the change but forge the path for others to follow. This is followed by the early adopters, then the majority (early and late) and finally laggards. Each group accepts and adopts the ideas over time until eventually, the market share becomes fully saturated.

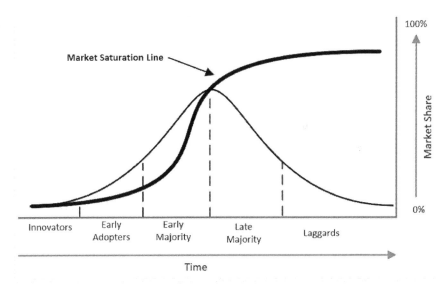

Figure 19: Diffusion of Innovation - Adapted from Diffusion of Innovations by Everett Rogers 1962

Transformation urgency

As always, IT continually changes. In today's IT world there are several reasons why there is an urgency for organizations to consider making transformational changes. These reasons can be broken into two primary groups, CX and technology drivers.

CX drivers

According to a recent study by Walker (Walkerinfo.com), CX is rapidly "becoming the number one driver of customers doing business with an organization." Walker's study shows a trend of purchasing decisions being directly attributed to CX. Their findings match and support the value statements I have been discussing throughout this book (i.e. the value is whatever a customer thinks it is).

According to the Walker study,

- 85% of buyers are willing to pay more for a better experience.
- 73% of buyers think CX is an important factor to purchasing.
- 56% of buyers find a positive experience more influential than great advertising.

These are impressive statistics and show just how customers are not only thinking about their choices but changing the core of how businesses work with their customers. Basically, customers are saying, "give me a great experience, or I will find someone else who will." Providing the lowest price to win new or keep existing business is no longer the only or even first priority consideration.

Organizations can and must address CX by placing the focus on their customers. Becoming customer-centric is no longer an afterthought or a nice characteristic to have in a company, it is a necessity. Organizations who miss or take too long to focus on this critical transformation driver will find themselves in trouble in the very near future.

Technology drivers

At first glance, it may seem to be just that, technology. However, upon a deeper inspection, you will find that all technologies really are driven by one of three underlying concerns... Better, Faster or Cheaper. Customers have always wanted all three of these from the products and services delivered by IT. As I have previously said, we in IT do a great job of the better and faster parts, but not so much in the cheaper. This push by customers to have companies provide services at a cheaper rate is the root reason in the urgency to change technology (the way we do business).

One of the buzzwords we hear lately is "disruptive innovation", where the creation of something new opens new markets or value and changes the way we have always done something in the past. IT disruptive innovation happens at breakneck speeds. With the advent of technologies such as cloud, artificial intelligence (AI), the internet (making the world more accessible) and a focus on CX, the IT world is not only changing faster than ever before, but changing at its core. Those organizations unable or unwilling to change with these innovations, will not be around for much longer. We have seen this in other industry segments, albeit at a much slower pace throughout history. For example, the typewriter industry. Typewriters preceded computers and were the way we wrote letters, general communications, forms etc. Then, when personal computers and printers came along, the typewriter days were numbered. We are in the midst of this type of disruptive innovation right now in IT.

Cloud technology has been around since the early 2000s, but in some cases was slow for companies to adopt because of security, cost or simply fear of losing control. Due to the cost pressures, cloud companies are addressing these issues and are becoming less of a risk for organizations.

Cloud computing's "as a service" technology stack covers Infrastructure as a Service (IaaS) – Network Infrastructure Services, Platform as a Service (PaaS) – Test and development services and Software as a Service (SaaS) – software application subscription services (Figure 20).

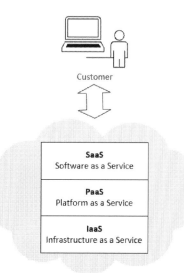

Figure 20: Cloud Technology Stack

With the increased maturity of security and reliability coupled with the business benefit of not overspending on unused capacity, each of these "as a service" models are gaining in popularity and market share. Cloud-based services are rapidly replacing the need to buy, own and maintain server hardware and data centers for organizations worldwide.

The internet has made our world a much smaller space. It has opened markets to companies that would have otherwise not had access to in the past. For example, if you wanted to buy a hammer, you went to your local hardware store. The e-commerce of the internet changed all that. Now you can buy hammers from anywhere in the world and have them shipped directly to you. This globalization applies to nearly any consumable these days from all types of products and services.

Automation and Artificial Intelligence (AI) technologies have been maturing at an exponential rate. For example, have you called any large organization lately? If so, you have probably received an interaction with an AI voice. It is a technology that asks you questions and listens to your response before directing solutions to your call, all without human interaction. Workforce automation is more than just entry-level, phone-based AI. It is the attempt and focus on automating pretty much anything that has a process. From backing up a server, extending a tablespace in a database or even automating the creation and delivery of application development efforts, workforce automation is making a huge impact in the way IT does its jobs and tasks.

Additionally, AI changes the risk for both employer and employee. For example, if a programmer completely automates every aspect of their job, is it ethical to not tell their employer and still charge the salary the organization provides? The work the company is paying for is being done, just not the way the employer thought it was. Is it wrong? In time companies will realize that AI will take over certain areas/functions and will pay to build, implement and maintain the AI, not the work the AI can do. Suffice to say, today's technology capabilities are increasing the ability to automate everything we do.

With all the technologies and globalization, competition is also on the rise. The ability for competitors to bring solutions to market is getting faster and cheaper. This competition is giving customers a lot more choices than they had in the past. Companies that keep doing things the way they always have, will find themselves losing business to competitors for many reasons.

Whether it's a natural progression or in response to the customer's demand for better *AND* faster *AND* cheaper (the old analogy - which came first, the chicken or the egg?), technologies are changing and becoming more global (e.g. cloud, software as a service, automation, artificial intelligence, etc.). Additionally, due to increased governance efforts, technologies are also more stable, secure and accepted at all levels.

This increased availability and stability have opened up new markets in the cloud and is disrupting the way IT and its customers do business. This has spurred both the creation, maturity, and acceptance of new ideas, methodologies, and processes including DevOps and Integrated Service Management.

Ultimately the drivers of and the change itself in the way IT provides services and products are vast and wide in scope. Troy DuMoulin of Pink Elephant describes this need for radical change as "the next major extinction event of IT." Those who do not rapidly adapt to meet customer needs will no longer be around.

Key Takeaways

- Better *AND* faster *AND* cheaper: Use what you already have in place.
- Innovation speeds to market saturation are becoming much shorter.
- CX is the largest factor for customer choices, not technology or money.
- Technology drivers are primarily driving cost reductions.
- Companies need to adapt quickly in creating a customer-centric culture.

CHAPTER 6:

COMMUNICATION FOR EVERYONE

Communication is one of those things we often take for granted. We automatically assume that everyone must know what we know. If we tell someone something, we expect them to understand completely (because we do) without further explanation. Can you remember a time where you explained something to a colleague, and they took what you said in a way that you did not expect and not what you intended? Of course, we all have.

Unfortunately, effective communication is a very elusive thing. For example, have you ever had a request from a manager to provide an explanation on how something functions or why a customer's ticket was "not handled properly?", and after the countless time and effort spent on creating the perfect email response, realize that the manager did not understand or even worse, never even looked at your email in the first place? Why is that?

Communication is so elusive because our ways of hearing, reading and understanding are based on many things including personal life experiences and (formal, informal or on-the-job) educational efforts about communication. Further complicating communication is the differences between the terminologies we use. For example, the term "incident" in ITSM's world means a disruption of normal services, however to HR it may mean a violation of a policy, while for Facilities it may mean something like a fire. As you can see, there are a lot of things to consider.

I remember a time early in my career where I was leading a team of desktop support staff. The organization's data center was located in the same building. The data center server's power supplies started failing at an increased rate. After several weeks of detailed troubleshooting, the root cause was determined to be zinc-whiskers being released into the data center every time a floor tile was removed/replaced to service the area below the raised floor. These zinc whiskers would float in the air, pushed around by the system fans and attach themselves to the power supply (and all other electrical) components, eventually shorting them out. The solution to this problem was to replace the raised floor. Unfortunately, this was the only data center for the organization, so they could not transfer the systems/data from this center to another. Instead, it was determined that the servers would be temporarily relocated to the desktop support team's build center for 2 weeks while the floor was being replaced.

My desktop team spent considerable amounts of time in the build center on a daily basis doing what desktop support staff do (e.g. building, repairing, troubleshooting, imaging, etc.). The project of replacing the floor fell behind schedule, as projects often do. First, it was communicated that it would just be a delay of one week, then two, four, and six weeks without an end in sight. After a few weeks of this, my staff began to complain about the conditions in the build center, increasing in lock step with the continued delays as the project became more and more protracted.

I held a team meeting, to understand all of the staff member's concerns so that I could take a summary of their complaints to management and resolve the issue long term. The primary concern brought up was the heat, which was caused by a lack of proper ventilation/refrigeration in the temporary space to accommodate all of the extra equipment. After the team went on about the heat for 45 minutes, one staff member raised another point. The team member said, "and it is loud too." I looked at him, surprised because he was correct, and no one had said anything about this point for weeks. My response to him was, "that's funny, I didn't even think of that." Now, let me be clear, I referred to the word "funny" to mean strange, and that it was interesting that we all seemed to have missed that point for so long. Unfortunately, the employee interpreted my statement as though I was laughing (in a joke sort of way) at his comments and didn't think the raised noise levels were of any consequence. After the meeting, he contacted the company's HR team and filed a formal complaint about my comment. What I thought was obvious, was not to everyone. What I thought was clear, was not to everyone. The key takeaway of this story is, even being in the same location having face-to-face interaction may not always be enough to ensure clear communication.

When I tell this story, I mostly get responses of "well, it's obvious that this employee over-reacted" or "why didn't he come to you as the supervisor rather than go to HR, it sounds like he just had an axe to grind." My response is always the same. It was my responsibility to ensure that everyone understood, was clear and on the same page. I failed the employee in this scenario by not being clear through the choice of my vocabulary and body language at the time. Yes, I could have taken the easy route and just chalked it up to a "disgruntled" employee and moved on, but in my opinion, because I was in a power position (as his manager) representing the organization, it was up to me to make sure I was being 100% clear and that everyone was on the same page. This was my failure, not the employee's. I learned from it and have tried hard not to repeat this type of miscommunication in all interactions ever since.

There are too many examples of these types of misunderstandings to go in this book. It is the subject of many books, films, and legends. One person meant one thing and others heard something else, next thing you know it's an all-out war. Suffice to say, words, written or verbal have many meanings and are taken out of context all the time. How you intend to say things aren't always the way that people perceive or understand them.

After the complaint, I spoke to the employee to clarify my meaning and the employee agreed it was a misunderstanding. We continued to work well together and be friendly for the rest of my tenure with the organization. Always look for the win, even if communication breaks down. The only way something remains a failure is if you don't take the initiative to bridge the gap and make sure everyone is on the same page.

3 Types of communication

There are three basic types of communication, *Verbal, Non-Verbal, and Written*. Verbal communication is the spoken language. Sometimes it's a face-to-face, sometimes not. Sometimes it's one way (e.g. a speech, a podcast, etc.), or it could be two way (e.g. a conversation). Non-verbal communication (e.g. body language, eye rolls, etc.) are the observations and interpretations of the messaging in a physical format. Written communication is just what it sounds like, written words in any format or method (e.g. books, newspapers, emails, notes, letters, instant message (IM) chats, etc.). Formal or informal.

We are all aware of these channels and use them in our own way at work every single day. Some people are long-winded, while some are concise, others prefer writing emails to phone calls, or prefer texts to any other method. The key to success in business communication is understating that everyone has their own way of communicating in each of these areas.

Communicating with Customers, Teams, Management, and Peers

Understanding your audience is vital to ensuring your message is successfully delivered and understood. If you communicate the same way to everyone, you may get your point across, but it will not be as effective, and increases the chances of misunderstanding.

To increase your chances of having both your communication heard and accurately understood, you should tailor your messages to the specific audience and use the methods they are most likely to use.

Customer Communication

Customer-centric organizations focus heavily on the perceptions of their customers and meeting their expectations. They are concerned with how, when, how often and to what extent the customer wants and needs to be communicated with. The best way to ensure that customer expectations are met is to ask them what they want to see, how they want to see it, how often, in how much or how little detail, etc. This is not a one-time ask either, it is never-ending.

Regularly checking with the customer directly and obtaining data points (survey responses, click through, email responses, etc.) is critical to ensuring that you are creating value for the customer as they perceive it. We often make the mistake in IT of defining the requirement, creating a solution and then assuming it will work like that or be important to the customer forever thereafter. The reality is things change, we need to work with the customers to regularly improve the communication and ensure we are meeting their needs.

Communication between teams

Communication between teams have always been a challenge in IT. This is because teams have a life of their owned, characterized by different experiences, backgrounds, and agendas. Teams goals and pressures to deliver coupled with individual concerns can add to a silo.

As discussed earlier in this book, to ensure an effective, customer-centric organization we must work to reduce and eliminate silos and the Wall of Confusion between IT teams. This all starts with reaching out to the other teams to understand their business, jobs, deliverables, etc. Once you understand this, and hopefully they understand your team, you can begin to build the connective communication tissue. For example, having people from both teams participating in meetings etc.

Two-way participation in meetings will also increase the trust of the team members, the teams themselves and ultimately increase value to the customer as well. In the end, we are all on the same team, trying to do the same thing, just in different ways. Working together is imperative to the success of everyone (Customer, Company, IT Organization, IT Team, and individual).

Communicating with organizational management

Successful communication with your manager(s) and/or management teams, requires that you understand their wants, needs, and expectations. Furthermore, you need to be able to apply your communication to these. For example, when communicating with executive level management, their time constraints typically require them to make rapid decisions. To their expectations, you need to get to your point faster and with more accuracy than when communicating with peers.

Getting to the point is a challenge for most of us in IT because everything is complicated, and we want to make sure the background, risks, and outcomes are well known so that the best possible decisions can be made. While I am not advocating you don't understand the details or that you don't provide it as a backup for your communication, I am suggesting you get to the point faster. You can always provide the details later or as an attachment if they want it. As a colleague of mine says "say less or talk faster." The bottom line is, when communicating with managers or executive management, you need to craft your message in a way that they will listen.

Peer Communication

Communicating with peers is typically the highest volume of communication occurring on a daily basis. These interactions create a bond of trust or (hopefully not) distrust between participants. Building and maintaining trust in these relationships is critical to everyone's success.

Remote/Virtual Team Communication

Technology has increased the ability and reliability of team members to work remotely, but this has also added another layer of complexity when communicating with and between these team members. While video conferences have also become mainstream and reliable, a lot of people don't like to use this technology for many reasons, including not wanting to see themselves on video. This leads to large periods of time where contact between team members are primarily conducted via chat, email or at best telephone.

To communicate successfully with remote users, the key is to set expectations with the team members early, check in with them often and never forget that nothing really replaces face-to-face interaction. Don't fall into the trap of out of sight, out of mind.

Tips for better communication

1. Keep it simple

This is a key tenet to the success of any communication. Shorter is better. But shorter is hard too. As Mark Twain said, "I didn't have time to write you a short Letter, so I wrote a long one instead." It takes a lot more effort to write something short rather than long. This is because you have to be precise with word usage to ensure clarity. Longer communications can meander, and through volume there is a hope for clarity.

Twitter has made us much better at thinking in short concise statements. The character limitation forces us to think about what we want to say and then cut out the unnecessary words. Why not apply this same methodology to your business communications? If your message is not compelling, too long, or confusing, it may not be read and/or understood as you would expect.

2. Common language

In my experience, successful communication is all about the audience, knowing what they want and how they prefer to communicate. If you know your audience, you can use their vocabulary, communication preferences, tools and technologies to boost your chances of successful communication.

3. Eliminate jargon

IT is famous for acronyms and technical jargon. While we work extremely hard to ensure we don't use this "technical speak" when communicating with users, we may occasionally catch ourselves doing it because it is used so freely inside the IT organization. It is sometimes hard to remember that not everyone has the same background, understanding or common language used inside our technical groups. Eliminate jargon and your communication efforts will produce better results for everyone.

4. Literacy levels

It is a well-known fact that newspapers in the United States write to a common literacy level between the 7th and 9th grade. The goal of this is to reach the largest audience possible and ensure the message is understood the same way for every reader. Taking this approach will help ensure your message is understood. There are even websites today where you can copy/paste a document and it will tell you the literacy level if you are so inclined. Write to a common literacy level to be more widely understood.

5. Communicate Early and Often

Communicating early and often is all about managing perceptions. I call it "paying it forward communication." It is the difference between reactionary and proactive. When communication is reactive, people have their guards up and are more likely to resist (intentionally or unintentionally) your message and the change. Proactive communication gives them the time to accept the message/change and prepare for them. Start communicating right away. Keep people updated and aware, before they reach out to you to ask what the status is and you will better meet their expectations.

6. Methods

During normal daily business, there are many opportunities to communicate and almost as many methods and channels to do so in. In my experience, face-to-face is better than a phone. The phone is better than email. Chat is better than email. Email is better than newsletters/blogs and newsletters/blogs are better than nothing. This may be different for you and your customers, so use what makes sense in your environment.

Recently, a lot of communication in the business world has been evolving from face-to-face to email notification, chat or text only to communicate important information to the organization. This is a challenge because it assumes people are reading these notifications. At best, it provides a repository of documentation for people to reference over time, and at worst is seen as an annoyance to the recipient. Further compounding the problem, there is really no way to measure the success of a chat/text/email/newsletter/blog unless an actual response is requested and/or required. For example, if you send a weekly newsletter describing changes to an organizational policy to all employees, the only thing that you can guarantee is how many emails were sent. Even if you require a read notification, there is no way to comprehend if someone actually read or understood your message. Therefore, these one-way communication methods are mainly documentation, not real communication.

While not everyone expects or communicates in the same way, it is important to understand that to avoid confusion and ensure your message is successful, the more senses (e.g. sight, sound, etc.) that are involved, the higher the probability of success.

I understand that not every communication can include all channels. Therefore, it is very critical that you understand the different audiences and have a common language, while continually checking in with your audiences to ensure the correct understanding of the message.

7. Communication Education

Communication methods, rules, and insights are constantly changing. Some of the core ideas remain the same, but technology and natural advancement of humanity will always drive improvements to yesterday and today's methods. Many studies have been conducted and books written about the most successful way to communicate. There are merit and value in all of them and I highly recommend you make studying effective communication a part of your ongoing lifelong learning process.

Key Takeaways

- Keep it simple.
- Speak a common language.
- Eliminate jargon.
- Communicate at the proper literacy level of the audience.
- Communicate early and often.

- Email, Newsletters, and blogs alone are a great backup to communication but are essentially only documentation.
- Don't assume your audience understands just because you do.

CHAPTER 7:

A WINNING STRATEGY FOR INTEGRATING ITSM

By far, culture is at the root of sustained success for any organization. Many companies have great ideas, services, products, offerings, etc. that initiate their business's success. Without these great ideas, the company would not exist at all in the first place: it is their culture that really makes the difference.

Culture, as I described in detail in Chapter 2, is how employees act when the boss is not around. It can either be purposefully cultivated, such as companies like Disney, Airbnb, and Zappos or organically grown without direction. Sometimes the organically grown culture works well, especially in a start-up organization because of the drive and focus of the initial staff, their desire to meet the needs of the customers are very strong. Left to chance, however, the possibility of a culture developing unintentionally, especially over time as new people come into the organization or new regulations and the organization's ultimate goals mature, can hinder or derail the success of an organization very quickly.

It is easier to identify, promote and drive the desired customer-centric culture in a startup organization than attempting to change and transform an existing one. Additionally, because culture is the way we do things, individual changes and developments occur over time, intended or not. It is very important that you not only identify, plan, promote and drive your desired customer-centric culture, but review and maintain it often to ensure it is continually moving and reflecting the direction you intend. I tell people all the time to develop their own career goals rather than relying on a supervisor to do it for them. If they don't, they may get to a point several years down where they are not happy in their position. It is better to get to your desired goal rather than one that is made for you. Similarly, I recommend developing your customer-culture, being very clear and living by it every day. Culture will happen, is it what you intended?

Often, we see an organization start, become successful, and grow substantially. Everyone loves to work for the company, customers love engaging with the company and then somewhere along the line, something changes. Whether its management change, financial pressures, or egotism, these companies become victims of their own success. Apple went through this when Steve Jobs was forced out in 1985, only ten years into Apple's lifespan after bringing in new CEO, John Sculley. Mr. Sculley came from Pepsi-Cola and refocused Apple's direction to be that of competition to IBM, the leader of computer sales at the time. Steve Jobs wanted to focus less on the hardware/software, and more on the outcome of what people could do with Apple products. With Sculley's direction change, the organization's culture also changed from a customer-centric model to a standard business model of profit and loss.

Apple's customer base was not interested in the normal. They were interested in the unique: as Steve Jobs put it, an "insanely great" experience that was curated in the first ten years, which people were willing to pay for. Sculley's direction, which was (and is still primarily) the standard business model way of working, made sense because his job was to make the business more profitable for investors. This did not really work because Apple wasn't in competition with the IBM. It had carved out a very unique space in the computer manufacturing space and customers loved it. Sculley's direction attempted to do the exact opposite of what caused Apple's success in the first place. They were different. They were not "big brother" and even made a television advertisement in 1984, referencing the "big brother" culture and inferring IBM that was a villain. Their customers loved it! After Mr. Sculley and Mr. Job's conflicts raised over direction and core business goals, Mr. Jobs exited Apple, leaving the chase to compete with IBM in full gear. The result was Apple's culture changed slowly, followed quickly by the decreased value the customers perceived and the company plunged to near extinction.

Unfortunately, as the success of the organization increased, so did the desire to run the it like every other company to gain growth and profit. The mentality was "do what any other successful company did, get what they got too." After all, this model was taught in business schools everywhere and had worked for many other large corporations. By following this model however, Apple forgot about their customers (or at least what they valued) and so began the downward spiral. Fortunately for Apple, Mr. Jobs came back just in time, refocusing on the customer and reinvigorating the culture that Apple was famous for. Customers followed, allowing Apple to regain its space as a market leader, proving that success is more than just profit, it's the culture that wins over dollarization.

Buy-in

There are two levels of buy-in I will discuss in this section, Executive Management and staff level. Executive managements buy-in because if they don't back your initiative, it will most likely fail since it won't get off the ground. Staff buy-in because if they don't back your initiative, it will fail due to fighting, sabotage, and resistance.

Executive level buy-in

According to research by Prosci (pronounced *pro-sigh)* a best practice research and consulting organization, the greatest contributor to overall change success is "Active and visible executive sponsorship." Knowing this, IT needs to seek out and gain buy-in and sponsorship from executive management before embarking on any change initiative.

Gaining executive buy-in is difficult sometimes, but the good news is there is a clear process to help. Just like we focus on our customers and the value they perceive, we focus on the executive leadership the same way, because after all, they are customers too. Start by finding out what the executives are concerned with, problems, and any ideas they have about the organization. As a general statement, executives are concerned with profitability (larger profits), growth (new business), retention of existing business (keep what you already have) and governance (staying out of jail). Then tailor your message to meet those needs.

Every executive is different, so please take this as a starting point for your efforts. Not every executive will feel the same about the items I discuss here. Suffice to say, you need to know your executives, what makes them tick, how they want to be communicated with, and what their biggest concerns are etc.

Staff buy-in

Staff buy-in begins by understanding your organization. Why are you (your department, etc.) there? What is your job? When I ask these questions, people often say "I'm a Desktop Support Agent" or some other technical job title. I know why they respond in this way. It is tied to how the business has grown and developed over time. No one has ever really come to them to explain that is how they provide value to a customer, but their actual job is helping their customer meet a business need. The best example I have heard of this is from a Hospital, where according to George Spalding of Pink Elephant, when IT staff members at all levels were asked why they were there (i.e. what their jobs were), they replied: "I save lives." This is a great response. It is the end game of IT to provide services and products to a user base to help them accomplish something. This is the difference between a typical mission/vision statement and the culture of the organization.

Once you truly understand your organization, what it does and why, the next step is to tie that to a very specific statement that means something to your customers and your team. When I speak with my teams about this, we try to make the statement as simple and clear as the "I save lives" example. Try this yourself. Try to create a compelling statement that uses three words or less (remember the Mark Twain quote from earlier about writing a short note?) to clearly describe why IT exists in your organization. It is harder than you think, but once complete, worth every second developing.

Now that you have the statement, the next step is to determine what needs to happen to get everyone on the same page, believing it with all their hearts. This is a change, so you will need to engage your organization change management skills. People must believe it. Many times, staff members hear of a change, but consistent action does not happen for long before reverting back to previous ways. You will need your executive management's buy-in and you need to be 100% consistent with this focus. Employees will "watch" across the organizations for this culture. If they see a wavering area away from the original goal, then the wavering becomes the new normal. No matter how small the item seems, it does have a rippling effect over time. You have to be diligent and protect your culture. It is the lifeblood of your organization and your differentiator. Remember, if you don't define, create and maintain it, the culture will gain a life of its own. To ensure it's the one you want, you must protect it.

Reinforcing the culture is critical in every communication channel in order to drive understanding and commitment. But you can't stop there. Just saying something is so, does not actually make it so. The staff knows this fact very well. If they see inconsistencies between what the culture initiatives are and the reality, then they will stop believing it and return to previous behaviors. The bottom line here is you need to walk the walk, not just talk the talk.

Continual Service Improvement (CSI)

Regardless of which CSI model you follow, the goal of CSI in a customer-centric model is to continually review and improve your services, processes or efforts to increase the value provided to the customer, better *AND* faster *AND* cheaper.

For CSI to work well, it needs to be designed into your entire organization, otherwise, it becomes an afterthought - a reactionary project after a failure or complaint. As we all know, afterthoughts rarely get done and a reactionary response is merely temporary band-aids. While you can't avoid problems from occurring entirely, you can proactively design the CSI process into each and every stage of your engagements.

CSI and documentation fall into this same category. Everyone "knows" these need to happen, but who has time? If anything else comes up, these are the two areas that are first to fall off the radar and the first to be chastised during root cause analysis and audits. The bottom line is if you focus on this as part of the job, don't ever waiver from the requirement, and follow up with staff constantly so it will get done. If you don't, it won't.

Strategy

The following strategy uses the three guiding principles for ensuring a successful IT transformation across the organization.

1. Communication is a key tenet to success
2. Leverage the existing frameworks, tools, and documentation
3. Keep it simple and _only_ focus on the activities that provide value to the customer

Guided by these principles, this strategy fully integrates CX, IT support services, and breaks down siloed support through efficiencies and scalability to ensure end users are kept as productive as possible. The four-step strategy includes all of the items discussed in this book.

Step 1: Gain executive buy-in

Success in this approach begins with gaining executive level engagement and sponsorship, providing consistent communication, determining appropriate methodology, ensuring properly resourced change support, and facilitating employee engagement.

Step 2: Create a CX Program

As CX is the primary differentiator, the next step is to design a program that includes VoC, Journey Mapping, and assessments. Your CX program should make things personal, easy to use and fast.

Step 3: Utilize Organizational Change (OC)

Employee engagement is key to the success of any organization. You must include them early and often in the changes that will affect them. If you do it after the change happens, it's too late. There are three specific areas in ensuring successful OC (see Figure 21):

1. *Preparing for change (unfreeze) – building the team, sponsorship, risk*
2. *Managing change (changing) – communication, training, monitoring*
3. *Reinforcing change (refreezing) – feedback, continual service improvement*

Unfreeze
Ensure readiness

Changing
Execution

Refreeze
Reinforce new norms

Figure 21: Kurt Lewin Change Model – Adapted from Lewin's 1947 paper, "Frontier in Group Dynamics".

Step 4: Engage Integrated Service Management

Don't reinvent the wheel, rather, adjust the methodologies and processes you already have to eliminate duplication of effort and ensure a customer-centric culture. Integrated Service Management provides value to the customer and meets the current and future challenges – ***better AND faster AND cheaper!***

- ITIL – Provides structure and definition
- Lean – Ensures continual improvement and process optimization
- Agile – Provides iterative project management
- DevOps – Unifies cross-functional culture, teaming and automation
- Organizational Change Management – Embeds culture and values

Key Takeaways

- Design, cultivate, consistently maintain and protect your culture, or it can become something you did not intend.
- Buy-in from Executives and Staff is required
- CSI is proactive. Reactionary is not customer-centric and at best, just irrevocable corrective actions
- CX
  o Culture shift to customer-focus
  o Break down silos, turn into journeys
  o Become an agile change organization
  o Make it personal
  o Make it easy
  o Reduce the process
  o Make it fast
- Integrated Service Management helps break down IT silos, increases the speed of service for customers, and reduces duplication of effort inside IT.

CONCLUSION

The future of ITSM is very bright. IT has come a long way over the years and still has a long way to go in order to reach its full potential. We are currently at a very critical point of disruptive innovation in the evolution of IT, where can make a substantial difference to how our world works for years to come. The exciting news is that we already have everything we need to ensure we provide the most value to customers. In order to stay relevant, IT must reinvent itself by creating a customer-centric model of support, engage its employees and utilize both new and existing technologies to meet customer and business needs now, and for the future. This is not an easy task, but by standardizing and consolidating different methodologies, IT can reduce costs while at the same time creating better and faster products and services for its customers.

Customers are the reason that IT exists. Everything we do must be focused on providing them with value. Remember, value is whatever the customer believes it to be. The only way to provide this is to ensure you know your customer, what they want, how they work, what they need and what is important to them. Using methods and tools like CX, VoC and journey mapping will help you document and better understand your customer's goals effectively and get all your people moving in the right direction towards a singular goal. Further, if customers are the reason we are here, then our staff and organizational culture are the lifeblood of the organization itself. Ensure you take care of your staff and protect the culture, or someone else will.

No change or transformation will be fully successful without executive buy-in. Changes can be successful from a grassroots perspective, but can only go so far, leading to silo-based support models. On the surface these silos may seem effective because they accomplish specific tasks for small groups, however when taken from an enterprise-wide initiative or customer's perspective of value, these silos can be seen for what they actually are: a costly duplication of effort, and conflicting priority hindrance for the full value expectation to the customer.

Organizational Change Management (OCM) is one of the most overlooked areas of IT and change. If we really want to succeed, we need to focus on our people long before we focus on the details or implementation of any change. Plan for success, communicate early and often, and prepare your teams and customers for the changes in a proactive manner - your success, or at least a reduction of resistance to any changes will occur. Reactive change is the norm for IT. If you want to increase your project completion success rates, make customers and staff happier, and reduce the overall time and costs of support, focusing instead on the proactive side of change with OCM.

Organizations adopt frameworks and best practices in an attempt to guarantee the quality of their services agreed with their clients. Today's focus on doing more with less drives the need to provide IT transformation in a way that facilitates Service Management in a better *AND* faster *AND* cheaper way. The good news is that everything we need is already in place. With ITIL is at its core of Integrated Service Management frameworks, practices and models are complementary to each other, providing a collaborative approach to technical service and support for both now and the future.

While ISM gives the main structure methodology behind the success of integrating service management, the underlying standards, model and best practices used to ensure governance, security and common practices (e.g. HDI, ISO, ISACA COBIT, NIST, etc.) should also be utilized to the extent that makes sense for your organization. Using everything in a consistent, but non-prescriptive manner will ensure you get the best value out of technology, methodologies, and structures. Consistency is the key to success, not forcibly instituting any specific tools, process or practice. Remember, the success is measured by how value is perceived by the customer. Value drives profitability, not the other way around.

Applying an Integrated Service Management approach, built on empowerment and collaboration with a customer-centric focus, results in a faster delivery, reduced costs of services, enhanced customer experience (CX), employee engagement and user satisfaction.

Key Takeaways

- The biggest challenge facing IT is the need to provide services to customers better *AND* faster *AND* cheaper.
- ITIL is at the core of Integrated Service Management and will continue to be a major part of the strategic response as IT responds to new challenges and ways of working.
- Integrated Service Management reduces legacy silo-based conflicting agendas, budgetary clashes, and duplication of effort, resulting in increased customer value and satisfaction.
- Integrated Service Management uses and realigns the strengths of existing groups, tools, technologies, frameworks and models to facilitate value through a customer-centric culture.
- As support organizations continually face increased mandates to consolidate and economize IT services, success requires leveraging cross-trained resources to optimize existing tools and technologies.
- First, understand who your customers are and what they value, then determine what is needed to facilitate the outcomes the customers want to achieve.
- Flattening the organization to deliver greater value to the customer requires commitment from the top management to drive an organizational culture change from IT to a customer-centric focus.
- It is essential to move solutions closer to the customer, creating a more positive support experience and meeting the expectations of receiving an immediate response more effectively.
- There is no one framework/model that will do or be it all. Integrated Service Management (ITIL, Lean, Agile, DevOps, and Organizational Change Management) are complementary to each other, providing a collaborative approach to technical service and support for both now and the future.

FURTHER READING

Creating a Lean Culture: Tools to Sustain Lean Conversions, Third Edition - David Mann

Lean Thinking: Banish Waste and Create Wealth in Your Corporation - James P. Womack, Daniel T. Jones

The Phoenix Project: A Novel about IT, DevOps, and Helping Your Business Win – Gene Kim and Kevin Behr

The DevOps Handbook: How to Create World-Class Agility, Reliability, and Security in Technology Organizations - Gene Kim, Jez Humble, Patrick Debois, John Willis, John Allspaw

The Effective Change Manager's Handbook: Essential Guidance to the Change Management Body of Knowledge - Nicola Busby, Richard Smith, David King, Ranjit Sidhu, Dan Skelsey

Managing Up: How to Move up, Win at Work, and Succeed with Any Type of Boss - Mary Abbajay

Happy R.A.V.I.N.G. Customers!: Six Powerful Steps to Grow Your Business with Exceptional Customer Experience - Carol Buehrens

Winning Minds: Secrets from the Language of Leadership - Simon Lancaster

The Intuitive Customer: 7 Imperatives for Moving Your Customer Experience to the Next Level - Colin Shaw, Ryan Hamilton

Chief Customer Officer 2.0: How to Build Your Customer-Driven Growth Engine - Jeanne Bliss

EXIN Agile Scrum Foundation Workbook - K. Rad, Nader; Turley, Frank

You've Got 8 Seconds Communication Secrets for a Distracted World - Paul Hellman

Customer Obsessed A Whole Company Approach to Delivering Exceptional Customer Experiences – Eric Berridge

How to Write Effective Business English Excel at E-mail, Social Media, and All Your Professional Communications, Second Edition - Fiona Talbot

Get to the Point!: Sharpen Your Message and Make Your Words Matter - Joel Schwartzberg

BRM Body of Knowledge – BRM Institute

ITIL Service Management Books (Service Strategy, Service Design, Service Transition, Service Operations, Continual Service Improvement, Managing across the Lifecycle) – Axelos

CX Primer – Nate Brown

Rise of the Customer Experience Executive - Annette Franz

REFERENCES

Chapter 1

Bolander, J. (2010, March 31). Topic #21: Organizational Structures. Retrieved November 3, 2018, from http://www.thedailymba.com/2010/03/24/topic-21-organizational-structures/

Alton, L. (2017, July 9). 4 Common Types of Organizational Structures. Retrieved November 3, 2018, from www.allbusiness.com/4-common-types-organizational-structures-103745-1.html

Karell, D. (2018, February 15). 4 Types of Organizational Structures. Retrieved November 3, 2018, from https://online.pointpark.edu/business/types-of-organizational-structures/

Devaney, E. (2017, July 28). An Illustrated Guide to Organizational Structures. Retrieved November 3, 2018, from https://blog.hubspot.com/marketing/illustrated-organizational-structures-guide

Brown, N (2018, January 23). The Ultimate Customer Experience prier. Retrieved November 4, 2018, from https://www.cxaccelerator.com/cxprimer

Customer Experience Professionals Association (2018). Retrieved November 4, 2018, from https://www.cxpa.org/home

ClearAction Continuum (2018). Retrieved November 4, 2018, from https://clearaction.com

CX Journey (2018). Retrieved November 4, 2018, from https://www.cx-journey.com/

Hunsaker, L. (2015, May 15). Customer Experience Governance. Do This, Not That. Retrieved November 4, 2018, from https://www.cxpa.org/blogs/lynn-hunsaker/2015/05/15/customer-experience-governance-do-this-not-that

Morris, H, Gallacher, L. (2016). ITIL Intermediate Certification Companion Study Guide: Intermediate ITIL Service Lifecycle Exams. Indianapolis: Sybex, John Wiley & Sons, Inc.

AXELOS (2011-07-29). ITIL Service Design (ITIL Lifecycle Suite). Norwich: TSO (The Stationery Office).

Chapter 2

Pohl, K., Böckle, G., van der Linden, F.J. (2005) Software Product Line Engineering: Foundations, Principles, and Techniques. Berlin, Heidelberg: Springer-Verlag

Womak, J. (2010). Lean Thinking: Banish Waste and Create Wealth in Your Corporation. New York: Free Press

Mann, D. (2014). Creating a Lean Culture: Tools to Sustain Lean Conversions. New York: Productivity Press

Bucheno, J. (2008). The Lean Toolbox for Service Systems. Buckinghamshire: Precise Books

Buehresns, C. (2018) Happy R.A.V.I.N.G. Customers! Six Powerful Steps to Grow Your Business with Exceptional Customer Experience. Scottsdale: MCH Press

Custom Insight contributors (2018). Employee Engagement Survey. Retrieved November 18, 2018, from https://www.custominsight.com/employee-engagement-survey/what-is-employee-engagement.asp

Wikipedia contributors. (2018 December 9). Design Thinking. Retrieved December 10, 2018, from https://en.wikipedia.org/wiki/Design_thinking

Gibbons, S. (2016 July 31). Design thinking 101. Retrieved January 15, 2019, from https://www.nngroup.com/articles/design-thinking/

Terrar, D. (2018 February 19). What is Design Thinking? Retrieved January 15, 2019, from https://www.enterpriseirregulars.com/125085/what-is-design-thinking/

Nasoi, R. (2017 August 23). 6 Customer Journey Mapping Examples: How UX Pros Do it. Retrieved January 15, 2019, from https://conversionxl.com/blog/customer-journey-mapping-examples/

Chapter 3

DuMoulin, T. (2017 November 21). The Case for Integrated Service Management. Retrieved November 4, 2018, from https://www.pinkelephantasia.com/case-integrated-service-management/

Womak, J. (2010). Lean Thinking: Banish Waste and Create Wealth in Your Corporation. New York: Free Press

Mann, D. (2014). Creating a Lean Culture: Tools to Sustain Lean Conversions. New York: Productivity Press

Bucheno, J. (2008). The Lean Toolbox for Service Systems. Buckinghamshire: Precise Books

Beck, K., Beedle, M., van Bennekum, A., Cockburn, A, Cunningham, W., Fowler, M., Grenning, J., Highsmith, J., Hunt, A., Jeffries, R., Kern, J., Marick, B., Martin, R.C. ,Mellor, S., Schwaber, K., Sutherland, J., Thomas, D. (2001 February 11). The Agile Manifesto. Retrieved November 8, 2018, from http://agilemanifesto.org/

K. Rad, Nader; Turley, F. (2014 October 28). EXIN Agile Scrum Foundation Workbook. Hertogenbosch: Van Haren Publishing.

Kim, G., Humble, J. Debois, P. Willis, J. Allspaw, J. (2016). The DevOps Handbook: How to Create World-Class Agility, Reliability, and Security in Technology Organizations: IT Revolution Press

Hiller, P., Kim, G. (2013 December 18). Gene Kim Defines the 3 Ways of The Phoenix Project. retrieved November 28, 2018, from https://www.youtube.com/watch?v=nUOXDEvplRc

Edwards, D. (2012 September 17). The (Short) History of DevOps. Retrieved 118/2018 from https://www.youtube.com/watch?v=o7-IuYS0iSE

Prosci Contributors (2018 November 13). Five Levers of Organizational Change Management. Retrieved November 13, 2018, from https://www.Prosci.com/resources/articles/five-levers-of-organizational-change-management

Business Relationship Management Institute contributors. (2018 November 18). BRMP Body of Knowledge [PDF]. retrieved November 18, 2018, from https://shop.brm.institute/product/brmp-guide/

ITChapter.com contributors. (2018 November 11). Top Five Things You Need To Know About Doing BRM The Right Way. Retrieved November 18, 2018, from https://itchapter.com/top5-brm

Goodreads.com contributors. (2018 November 11). Abraham Lincoln: John Lydgate > Quotes > Quotable Quote. Retrieved November 11, 2018, from https://www.goodreads.com/quotes/699462-you-can-please-some-of-the-people-all-of-the

Zhuk, A. (2018 November 18). Business Relationship Management (BRM) – in 3 minutes. Retrieved 11/18/2018 from http://www.vanharen.net/blog/business-management/business-relationship-management-brm-in-3-minutes/

Pink Elephant Contributors (2018 November 13). Integrated Service Management. Retrieved November 4, 2018, from https://www.pinkelephant.com/en-us/Certifications/Integrated-Service-Management

Prosci Contributors (2018 November 14). Tips for Managing Resistance to Change. Retrieved November 14, 2018, from https://www.Prosci.com/resources/articles/tips-for-managing-resistance-to-change

Kübler-Ross, E. (2014). On Grief and Grieving: Finding the Meaning of Grief Through the Five Stages of Loss. New York: Scribner

NIST contributors. (2018 May 21). NIST Special Publication 800-series General Information. retrieved November 18, 2018, from https://www.nist.gov/itl/nist-special-publication-800-series-general-information

CMMI Institute. (2018 November 21). Retrieved November 21, 2018, from https://cmmiinstitute.com/

Suchi. (2017 May 22). 5 Ways To Achieve CMMI Level 3 Certification For Any Organization. Retrieved November 21, 2018, from https://www.cunixinfotech.com/5-ways-achieve-cmmi-level-3-certification-organization/

Griffen, S. (2019 January 4). What Are The 9 Guiding Principles Of ITIL®? Retrieved January 15, 2019, from https://purplegriffon.com/blog/9-guiding-principles-ITIL

Rivers, A. (2019 January 1). What is the ITIL©v4 Service Value Chain? Retrieved from https://www.beyond20.com/blog/what-is-the-itil-4-service-value-chain/

Chapter 4

International Organization for Standardization. (2018 November 18). ISO 9001:2015. Retrieved November 18, 2018, from https://www.iso.org/iso-9001-quality-management.html

International Organization for Standardization. (2018 November 18). ISO 9001:2015. Retrieved November 18, 2018, from https://www.iso.org/standard/62085.html

International Organization for Standardization. (2018 November 18). ISO/IEC 20000-1:2018. Retrieved November 18, 2018, from https://www.iso.org/standard/70636.html 11/18/2018

International Organization for Standardization. (2017 December 12). Retrieved December 12, 2018, from https://www.iso.org/isoiec-27001-information-security.html

International Organization for Standardization. (2019 January 14). ISo/IEC 27002. Retrieved January 14, 2019, from http://www.iso27001security.com/html/27002.html

International Organization for Standardization. (2018 November 18). ISO/IEC 15504-1:2004. Retrieved November 18, 2018, https://www.iso.org/standard/38932.html

ISACA contributors. (2019 January 15). COBIT 2019. Retrieved January 15, 2019, from https://www.isaca.org/cobit/pages/default.aspx.

itservicemngmt.blogspot.com Contributors. (2012 April 18) ISO 9000 - ISO/IEC 27001 - ISO/IEC 20000: How do They Fit Together? Retrieved November 18, 2018, from http://itservicemngmt.blogspot.com/2012/04/iso-isoiec-27001-isoiec-20000-how-do.html

Nicho, M., Khan, S. Rahman, M.S.M.K. (2017 October 26). Managing information security risk using Integrated Governance risk and compliance. Retrieved November 18, 2018, from https://openair.rgu.ac.uk/bitstream/handle/10059/2315/NICHO%202017%20Managaing%20Risk%20using%20Integrated%20Governance.pdf?sequence=5&isAllowed=y

International Organization for Standardization. (2018 November 18). ISO/IEC 38500. Retrieved November 18, 2018, from https://www.iso.org/standard/62816.html

Bırakın, Y. (2015 March 27). The relation between ITIL, Cobit, Togaf, and CMMI. retrieved November 21, 2018, from https://smtakar.wordpress.com/2015/03/27/relation-in-between-itil-cobit-togaf-and-cmmi/

CMMI Institute. (2018 November 21). Retrieved November 21, 2018, from https://cmmiinstitute.com/

Suchi. (2017 May 22). 5 Ways To Achieve CMMI Level 3 Certification For Any Organization. Retrieved November 21, 2018, from https://www.cunixinfotech.com/5-ways-achieve-cmmi-level-3-certification-organization/

HDI. (2018 November 11). Website. Retrieved November 21, 2018, from https://www.thinkhdi.com

HDI Contributor. (2018 November 21). The Importance of a Consistent Customer Experience: A Case Study. Retrieved November 210, 2018, from https://www.thinkhdi.com/events/awards/team-certified/NuAxis-Team-Certified-Pinnacle-of-Excellence-Award

International Organization for Standardization. (2018 November 18). Website. Retrieved November 21, 2018, from https://www.iso.org/home.html

International Organization for Standardization. (2018 November 18). Website. Retrieved November 21, 2018, from https://www.iso.org/home.html

NIST contributors. (2018 November 21). Cybersecurity Framework. retrieved November 21, 2018, from https://www.nist.gov/cyberframework

itSM Solutions NISTCSF.COM. (2018 November 21). NIST Cybersecurity Certification Training. Retrieved November 11, 2018, from https://nistcsf.com/register-for-nist-cybersecurity-training/

Project Management Institute. (2018 November 21). Website. retrieved November 21, 2018, from https://www.pmi.org/

Vizteams contributors. (2013 July 12). Tip 6 Benefits of Adopting CMMI Framework. Retrieved January 15, 2019, from https://www.vizteams.com/blog/top-6-benefits-of-adopting-capability-maturity-model-cmmi-focus-software-companies/

International Organization for Standardization. (2015). Reaping the Benefits of ISO 9001. Retrieved January 15, 2019, from https://www.iso.org/files/live/sites/isoorg/files/archive/pdf/en/reaping_the_benefits_of_iso_9001.pdf

NITS.gov. (2018 February 6). Uses and Benefits of the Framework. Retrieved January 15, 2019, from https://www.nist.gov/cyberframework/online-learning/uses-and-benefits-framework

Wilson, L. (2018 October 2). Designing a Cybersecurity Program based on the NIST Cybersecurity Framework. Retrieved October 2, 2018, from itSMFUSA Fusion18

Chapter 5

BRMInstitute.com contributors. (2018 December 6). Business Relationship Management Executive Brief. Retrieved December 6, 2018, from https://brm.institute/professional-development/business-relationship-management-executive-brief/

Rogers, E.M. (2003). Diffusion of Innovations. New York: Free Press

Kulbyte, T. (2018 November 29). 35 Customer Experience Statistics You Need to Know for 2019. Retrieved December 7, 2018, from https://www.superoffice.com/blog/customer-experience-statistics/

Walker contributors. (2013, 2018 December 7) Customers 2020: A Progress Report, Retrieved December 7, 2018, from https://www.walkerinfo.com/knowledge-center/featured-research-reports/customers-2020-a-progress-report

CXPA website. (2013, 2018 December 7) Customers 2020: More Insight for a New Decade, Retrieved December 7, 2018, from https://www.cxpa.org/HigherLogic/System/DownloadDocumentFile.ashx?DocumentFileKey=256e746b-7a5f-9d49-c63f-c651657db9e9

DuMoulin, T. (2017 November 21). The Case for Integrated Service Management. Retrieved November 4, 2018, from https://www.pinkelephantasia.com/case-integrated-service-management/

Amazon contributors. (2019 January 15). What is Cloud Computing? Retrieved January 15, 2019, from https://aws.amazon.com/what-is-cloud-computing/

DuMoulin, T. (2017). Critical Success factors for DevOps. Retrieved December 10, 2018, from https://www1.pinkelephant.com/PinkLINK/na/issue199/Critical-Success-Factors-For-DevOps.pdf

Bhatnagar, K (2012). Customer-Oriented Global Supply Chains: Concepts for Effective Management. Hershey, Pennsylvania: Information Science Reference.

Saban, A.K.; Mawhinney, J (2012). Customer-Oriented Global Supply Chains: Concepts for Effective Management. Hershey, Pennsylvania: Information Science Reference.

Kolakowski, N. (2018 October 9). Is It Ethical to Automate Your Job Without Telling Anyone? Retrieved December 7, 2018, from https://insights.dice.com/2018/10/09/is-it-ethical-to-automate-your-job-without-telling-anyone/

Christensen, C. (2005 December 31). The Encyclopedia of Human-Computer Interaction, 2nd Ed., chapter 17. Disruptive Innovation. Retrieved January 15, 2019, from https://www.interaction-design.org/literature/book/the-encyclopedia-of-human-computer-interaction-2nd-ed/disruptive-innovation

Chapter 6

Hartzell, S. (2018 November 18). Types of Communication: Interpersonal, Non-Verbal, Written & Oral. Retrieved November 18, 2018, from https://study.com/academy/lesson/types-of-communication-interpersonal-non-verbal-written-oral.html

Goodreads.com. (2018 December 10). Mark Twain Quote. Retrieved December 12, 2018, from https://www.goodreads.com/quotes/21422-i-didn-t-have-time-to-write-a-short-letter-so

Harvard Business Review contributors. (2018 November 18). Communication. Retrieved November 18, 2018, from https://hbr.org/topic/communication 11/18/2018

DuBay, W. (2018 December 5). Know your readers. Retrieved December 5, 2018, from http://www.impact-information.com/impactinfo/literacy.htm

Chapter 7

Winfrey, G. (2015 December 17). Why Steve Jobs Left Apple 30 Years Ago Today. retrieved December 6, 2018, from https://www.inc.com/graham-winfrey/why-steve-jobs-left-apple-30-years-ago-today.html

Russell, K. (2108 December 6) 25 Steve Jobs Quotes That Will Change the Way You Work—in the Best Way Possible. Retrieved December 6, 2018, from https://www.themuse.com/advice/25-steve-jobs-quotes-that-will-change-the-way-you-workin-the-best-way-possible

ACCIPIO contributors. (2016 May 31). Kurt Lewin's Three-Step Change Model. Retrieved December 10, 2018, from https://www.accipio.com/eleadership/mod/wiki/view.php?id=1873

Hintz, E. (22 January 2014) Remembering Apple's "1984" Super Bowl ad. Retrieved January 15, 2019, from http://americanhistory.si.edu/blog/2014/01/remembering-apples-1984-super-bowl-ad.html

ABOUT THE AUTHOR

Bob is a results-driven Service Management and Leadership executive with an unwavering focus on delivering world-class customer and employee satisfaction. With a broad range of technical and business experience across multiple industries, his positive approach of empowering, coaching and developing colleagues drives business value for all stakeholders through a culture of collaboration and customer-centricity.

Bob is an MBA graduate of Western Governors University, recipient of a CX Impact Award for Outstanding Professionals from the Customer Experience Professionals Association (CXPA), AXELOS Ambassador, bestselling author, speaker, trainer, and recognized as one of America's PremierExperts™. Bob also holds numerous industry-leading certifications including ITIL v3 Expert, CCXP, PMP, HDI SCD, and BRMP.

You can connect with Bob at:
www.bobroark.com
www.linkedin.com/in/bobroark
www.twitter.com/bobroarkdotcom

Made in the USA
Columbia, SC
12 March 2019